# The Storm-Cloud
# Nineteenth Century

John Ruskin

**Alpha Editions**

This edition published in 2024

ISBN : 9789362925732

Design and Setting By
**Alpha Editions**
www.alphaedis.com
Email - info@alphaedis.com

As per information held with us this book is in Public Domain.
This book is a reproduction of an important historical work. Alpha Editions uses the best technology to reproduce historical work in the same manner it was first published to preserve its original nature. Any marks or number seen are left intentionally to preserve its true form.

# PREFACE.

The following lectures, drawn up under the pressure of more imperative and quite otherwise directed work, contain many passages which stand in need of support, and some, I do not doubt, more or less of correction, which I always prefer to receive openly from the better knowledge of friends, after setting down my own impressions of the matter in clearness as far as they reach, than to guard myself against by submitting my manuscript, before publication, to annotators whose stricture or suggestion I might often feel pain in refusing, yet hesitation in admitting.

But though thus hastily, and to some extent incautiously, thrown into form, the statements in the text are founded on patient and, in all essential particulars, accurately recorded observations of the sky, during fifty years of a life of solitude and leisure; and in all they contain of what may seem to the reader questionable, or astonishing, are guardedly and absolutely true.

In many of the reports given by the daily press, my assertion of radical change, during recent years, in weather aspect was scouted as imaginary, or insane. I am indeed, every day of my yet spared life, more and more grateful that my mind is capable of imaginative vision, and liable to the noble dangers of delusion which separate the speculative intellect of humanity from the dreamless instinct of brutes: but I have been able, during all active work, to use or refuse my power of contemplative imagination, with as easy command of it as a physicist's of his telescope: the times of morbid are just as easily distinguished by me from those of healthy vision, as by men of ordinary faculty, dream from waking; nor is there a single fact stated in the following pages which [iv] I have not verified with a chemist's analysis, and a geometer's precision.

The first lecture is printed, with only addition here and there of an elucidatory word or phrase, precisely as it was given on the 4th February. In repeating it on the 11th, I amplified several passages, and substituted for the concluding one, which had been printed with accuracy in most of the leading journals, some observations which I thought calculated to be of more general interest. To these, with the additions in the first text, I have now prefixed a few explanatory notes, to which numeral references are given in the pages they explain, and have arranged the fragments in connection clear enough to allow of their being read with ease as a second Lecture.

HERNE HILL, *12th March, 1884.*

# LECTURE I

Let me first assure my audience that I have no *arrière pensée* in the title chosen for this lecture. I might, indeed, have meant, and it would have been only too like me to mean, any number of things by such a title;—but, to-night, I mean simply what I have said, and propose to bring to your notice a series of cloud phenomena, which, so far as I can weigh existing evidence, are peculiar to our own times; yet which have not hitherto received any special notice or description from meteorologists.

So far as the existing evidence, I say, of former literature can be interpreted, the storm-cloud—or more accurately plague-cloud, for it is not always stormy—which I am about to describe to you, never was seen but by now living, or *lately* living eyes. It is not yet twenty years that this—I may well call it, wonderful, cloud has been, in its essence, recognizable. There is no description of it, so far as I have read, by any ancient observer. Neither Homer nor Virgil, neither Aristophanes nor Horace, acknowledge any such clouds among those compelled by Jove. Chaucer has no word of them, nor Dante;[1] Milton none, nor Thomson. In modern times, Scott, Wordsworth and Byron are alike unconscious of them; and the most observant and descriptive of scientific men, De Saussure, is utterly silent concerning them. Taking up the traditions of air from the year before Scott's death, I am able, by my own constant and close observation, to certify you that in the forty following years (1831 to 1871 approximately—for the phenomena in question came on gradually)—no such clouds as these are, and are now often for months without intermission, were ever seen in the skies of England, France, or Italy.

In those old days, when weather was fine, it was luxuriously fine; when it was bad—it was often abominably bad, but it had its fit of temper and was done with it—it didn't sulk for three months without letting you see the sun,—nor send you one cyclone inside out, every Saturday afternoon, and another outside in, every Monday morning.

In fine weather the sky was either blue or clear in its light; the clouds, either white or golden, adding to, not abating, the luster of the sky. In wet weather, there were two different species of clouds,—those of beneficent rain, which for distinction's sake I will call the non-electric rain-cloud, and those of storm, usually charged highly with electricity. The beneficent rain-cloud was indeed often extremely dull and gray for days together, but gracious nevertheless, felt to be doing good, and often to be delightful after drought; capable also of the most exquisite coloring, under certain conditions;[2] and continually traversed in clearing by the rainbow:—and, secondly, the storm-cloud, always majestic, often dazzlingly beautiful, and felt also to be beneficent in its own way, affecting the mass of the air with vital agitation, and purging it from the impurity of all morbific elements.

In the entire system of the Firmament, thus seen and understood, there appeared to be, to all the thinkers of those ages, the incontrovertible and unmistakable evidence of a Divine Power in creation, which had fitted, as the air for human breath, so the clouds for human sight and nourishment;—the Father who was in heaven feeding day by day the souls of His children with marvels, and satisfying them with bread, and so filling their hearts with food and gladness.

Their *hearts*, you will observe, it is said, not merely their bellies,—or indeed not at all, in this sense, their bellies—but the heart itself, with its blood for this life, and its faith for the next. The opposition between this idea and the notions of our own time may be more accurately expressed by modification of the Greek than of the English sentence. The old Greek is—

ἐμπιπλῶν τροφῆς καὶ εὐφροσύνης
τὰς καρδίας ἡμῶν.

filling with meat, and cheerfulness, our hearts. The modern Greek should be—

ἐμπιπλῶν ἀνέμου καὶ ἀφροσύνης
τὰς γαστέρας ἡμῶν.

filling with wind, and foolishness, our stomachs.

You will not think I waste your time in giving you two cardinal examples of the sort of evidence which the higher forms of literature furnish respecting the cloud-phenomena of former times.

When, in the close of my lecture on landscape last year at Oxford, I spoke of stationary clouds as distinguished from passing ones, some blockheads wrote to the papers to say that clouds never were stationary. Those foolish letters were so far useful in causing a friend to write me the pretty one I am about to read to you, quoting a passage about clouds in Homer which I had myself never noticed, though perhaps the most beautiful of its kind in the Iliad. In the fifth book, after the truce is broken, and the aggressor Trojans are rushing to the onset in a tumult of clamor and charge, Homer says that the Greeks, abiding them "stood like clouds." My correspondent, giving the passage, writes as follows:—

"SIR,—Last winter when I was at Ajaccio, I was one day reading Homer by the open window, and came upon the lines—

Ἀλλ' ἔμενον, νεφέλῃσιν ἐοικότες ἅς τε Κρονίων
Νηνεμίης ἔστησεν ἐπ' ἀκροπόλοισιν ὄρεσσιν,
Ἀτρέμας, ὄφρ' εὕδῃσι μένος Βορέαο καὶ ἄλλων
Ζαχρειῶν ἀνέμων, οἵ τε νέφεα σκιόεντα
Πνοιῇσιν λιγυρῇσι διασκιδνᾶσιν ἀέντες·
Ὣσ Δαναοὶ Τρῶας μένον ἔμπεδον, οὐδ' ἐφέβοντο.

'But they stood, like the clouds which the Son of Kronos stablishes in calm upon the mountains, motionless, when the rage of the North and of all the fiery winds is asleep.' As I finished these lines, I raised my eyes, and looking across the gulf, saw a long line of clouds resting on the top of its hills. The day was windless, and there they stayed, hour after hour, without any stir or motion. I remember how I was delighted at the time, and have often since that day thought on the beauty and the truthfulness of Homer's simile.

"Perhaps this little fact may interest you, at a time when you are attacked for your description of clouds.

"I am, sir, yours faithfully,
G. B. HILL."

With this bit of noonday from Homer, I will read you a sunset and a sunrise from Byron. That will enough express to you the scope and sweep of all glorious literature, from the orient of Greece herself to the death of the last Englishman who loved her.[3] I will read you from 'Sardanapalus' the address of the Chaldean priest Beleses to the sunset, and of the Greek slave, Myrrha, to the morning.

"The sun goes down: methinks he sets more slowly,
Taking his last look of Assyria's empire.
How red he glares amongst those deepening clouds,[4]
Like the blood he predicts.[5] If not in vain,
Thou sun that sinkest, and ye stars which rise,
I have outwatch'd ye, reading ray by ray
The edicts of your orbs, which make Time tremble
For what he brings the nations, 't is the furthest
Hour of Assyria's years. And yet how calm!
An earthquake should announce so great a fall—
A summer's sun discloses it. Yon disk
To the star-read Chaldean, bears upon
Its everlasting page the end of what
Seem'd everlasting; but oh! thou TRUE sun!
*The burning oracle of all that live,*

*As fountain of all life*, and *symbol of*
*Him who bestows it*, wherefore dost thou limit
Thy lore unto calamity?[6] Why not
Unfold the rise of days more worthy thine
All-glorious burst from ocean? why not dart
A beam of hope athwart the future years,
As of wrath to its days? Hear me! oh, hear me!
I am thy worshiper, thy priest, thy servant—
I have gazed on thee at thy rise and fall,
And bow'd my head beneath thy mid-day beams,
When my eye dared not meet thee. I have watch'd
For thee, and after thee, and pray'd to thee,
And sacrificed to thee, and read, and fear'd thee,
And ask'd of thee, and thou hast answer'd—but
Only to thus much. While I speak, he sinks—
Is gone—and leaves his beauty, not his knowledge,
To the delighted west, which revels in
Its hues of dying glory. Yet what is
Death, so it be but glorious? 'T is a sunset;
And mortals may be happy to resemble
The gods but in decay."

Thus the Chaldean priest, to the brightness of the setting sun. Hear now the Greek girl, Myrrha, of his rising.

"The day at last has broken. What a nightHath usher'd it! How beautiful in heaven!Though varied with a transitory storm,More beautiful in that variety:[7]How hideous upon earth! where peace, and hope,And love, and revel, in an hour were trampledBy human passions to a human chaos,Not yet resolved to separate elements:—'T is warring still! And can the sun so rise,So bright, so rolling back the clouds into*Vapors more lovely than the unclouded sky,*With golden pinnacles, and snowy mountains,And billows purpler than the ocean's, makingIn heaven a glorious mockery of the earth,So like,—we almost deem it permanent;So fleeting,—we can scarcely call it aughtBeyond a vision, 't is so transientlyScatter'd along the eternal vault: and yetIt dwells upon the soul, and soothes the soul,And blends itself into the soul, untilSunrise and sunset form the haunted epochOf sorrow and of love."

How often *now*—young maids of London,—do you make *sunrise* the 'haunted epoch' of either?

Thus much, then, of the skies that used to be, and clouds "more lovely than the unclouded sky," and of the temper of their observers. I pass to the account of clouds that *are*, and—I say it with sorrow—of the *di*stemper of *their* observers.

But the general division which I have instituted between bad-weather and fair-weather clouds must be more carefully carried out in the sub-species, before we can reason of it farther: and before we begin talk either of the sub-genera and sub-species, or super-genera and super-species of cloud, perhaps we had better define what *every* cloud is, and must be, to begin with.

Every cloud that can be, is thus primarily definable: "Visible vapor of water floating at a certain height in the air." The second clause of this definition, you see, at once implies that there is such a thing as visible vapor of water which does *not* float at a certain height in the air. You are all familiar with one extremely cognizable variety of that sort of vapor—London Particular; but that especial blessing of metropolitan society is only a strongly-developed and highly-seasoned condition of a form of watery vapor which exists just as generally and widely at the bottom of the air, as the clouds do—on what, for convenience' sake, we may call the top of it;—only as yet, thanks to the sagacity of scientific men, we have got no general name for the bottom cloud, though the whole question of cloud nature begins in this broad fact, that you have one kind of vapor that lies to a certain depth on the ground, and another that floats at a certain height in the sky. Perfectly definite, in both cases, the surface level of the earthly vapor, and the roof level of the heavenly vapor, are each of them drawn within the depth of a fathom. Under *their* line, drawn for the day and for the hour, the clouds will not stoop, and above *theirs,* the mists will not rise. Each in their own region, high or deep, may expatiate at their pleasure; within that, they climb, or decline,—within that they congeal or melt away; but below their assigned horizon the surges of the cloud sea may not sink, and the floods of the mist lagoon may not be swollen.

That is the first idea you have to get well into your minds concerning the abodes of this visible vapor; next, you have to consider the manner of its visibility. Is it, you have to ask, with cloud vapor, as with most other things, that they are seen when they are there, and not seen when they are not there? or has cloud vapor so much of the ghost in it, that it can be visible or invisible as it likes, and may perhaps be all unpleasantly and malignantly there, just as much when we don't see it, as when we do? To which I answer, comfortably and generally, that, on the whole, a cloud is where you see it, and isn't where you don't; that, when there's an evident and honest thundercloud in the northeast, you needn't suppose there's a surreptitious and slinking one in the northwest;—when there's a visible fog at Bermondsey, it doesn't follow there's a spiritual one, more than usual, at the West End: and when you get up to the clouds, and can walk into them or out of them, as you like, you find when you're in them they wet your whiskers, or take out your curls, and when you're out of them, they don't; and therefore you may with probability assume—not with certainty, observe, but with probability—that there's more water in the air where it damps your curls than where it doesn't. If it gets much denser than that, it will begin to rain; and then you may assert, certainly with safety, that there is a shower in one place, and not in another; and not allow the scientific people to tell you that the rain is everywhere, but palpable in Tooley Street, and impalpable in Grosvenor Square.

That, I say, is broadly and comfortably so on the whole,—and yet with this kind of qualification and farther condition in the matter. If you watch the steam coming strongly out of an engine-funnel,[8]—at the top of the funnel it is transparent,—you can't see it, though it is more densely and intensely there than anywhere else. Six inches out of the funnel it becomes snow-white,—you see it, and you see it, observe, exactly where it is,—it is then a real and proper cloud. Twenty yards off the funnel it scatters and melts away; a little of it sprinkles you with rain if you are underneath it, but the rest disappears; yet it is still there;—the surrounding air does not absorb it all into space in a moment; there is a gradually diffusing current of invisible moisture at the end of the visible stream—an invisible, yet quite substantial, vapor; but not, according to our definition, a cloud, for a cloud is vapor *visible*.

Then the next bit of the question, of course, is, What makes the vapor visible, when it is so? Why is the compressed steam transparent, the loose steam white, the dissolved steam transparent again?

The scientific people tell you that the vapor becomes visible, and chilled, as it expands. Many thanks to them; but can they show us any reason why particles of water should be more opaque when they are separated than when they are close together, or give us any idea of the difference of the state of a particle of water, which won't *sink* in the air, from that of one that won't *rise* in it?[9]

And here I must parenthetically give you a little word of, I will venture to say, extremely useful, advice about scientific people in general. Their first business is, of course, to tell you things that are so, and do happen,—as that, if you warm water, it will boil; if you cool it, it will freeze; and if you put a candle to a cask of gunpowder, it will blow you up. Their second, and far more important business, is to tell you what you had best do under the circumstances,—put the kettle on in time for tea; powder your ice and salt, if you have a mind for ices; and obviate the chance of explosion by not making the gunpowder. But if, beyond this safe and beneficial business, they ever try to *explain* anything to you, you may be confident of one of two things,—either that they know nothing (to speak of) about it, or that they have only seen one side of it—and not only haven't seen, but usually have no mind to see, the other. When, for instance, Professor Tyndall explains the twisted beds of the Jungfrau to you by intimating that the Matterhorn is growing flat;[10] or the clouds on the lee side of the Matterhorn by the wind's rubbing against the windward side of it,[11]—you may be pretty sure the scientific people don't know much (to speak of) yet, either about rock-beds, or cloud-beds. And even if the explanation, so to call it, be sound on one side, windward or lee, you may, as I said, be nearly certain it won't do on the other. Take the very top and center of scientific interpretation by the greatest of its masters: Newton explained to you—or at least was once supposed to have explained—why an apple fell; but he never thought of explaining the exactly correlative, but infinitely more difficult question, how the apple got up there!

You will not, therefore, so please you, expect me to explain anything to you,—I have come solely and simply to put before you a few facts, which you can't see by candlelight, or in railroad tunnels, but which are making themselves now so very distinctly felt as well as seen, that you may perhaps have to roof, if not wall, half London afresh before we are many years older.

I go back to my point—the way in which clouds, as a matter of fact, become visible. I have defined the floating or sky cloud, and defined the falling, or earth cloud. But there's a sort of thing between the two, which needs a third definition: namely, Mist. In the 22d page of his 'Glaciers of the Alps,' Professor Tyndall says that "the marvelous blueness of the sky in the earlier part of the day indicated that the air was charged, almost to saturation, with transparent aqueous vapor." Well, in certain weather that is true. You all know the peculiar clearness which precedes rain,—when the distant hills are looking nigh. I take it on trust from the scientific people that there is then a quantity—almost to saturation—of aqueous vapor in the air, but it is aqueous vapor in a state which makes the air more transparent than it would be without it. What state of aqueous molecule is that, absolutely unreflective[12] of light—perfectly transmissive of light, and showing at once the color of blue water and blue air on the distant hills?

I put the question—and pass round to the other side. Such a clearness, though a certain forerunner of rain, is not always its forerunner. Far the contrary. Thick air is a much more frequent forerunner of rain than clear air. In cool weather, you will often get the transparent prophecy: but in hot weather, or in certain not hitherto defined states of atmosphere, the forerunner of rain is mist. In a general way, after you have had two or three days of rain, the air and sky are healthily clear, and the sun bright. If it is hot also, the next day is a little mistier—the next misty and sultry,—and the next and the next, getting thicker and thicker—end in another storm, or period of rain.

I suppose the thick air, as well as the transparent, is in both cases saturated with aqueous vapor;—but also in both, observe, vapor that floats everywhere, as if you mixed mud with the sea; and it takes no shape anywhere: you may have it with calm, or with wind, it makes no difference to it. You have a nasty haze with a bitter east wind, or a nasty haze with not a leaf stirring, and you may have the clear blue vapor with a fresh rainy breeze, or the clear blue vapor as still as the sky above. What difference is there between *these* aqueous molecules that are clear, and those that are muddy, *these* that must sink or rise, and those that must stay where they are, *these* that have form and stature, that are bellied like whales and backed like weasels, and those that have neither backs nor fronts, nor feet nor faces, but are a mist—and no more—over two or three thousand square miles?

I again leave the questions with you, and pass on.

Hitherto I have spoken of all aqueous vapor as if it were either transparent or white—visible by becoming opaque like snow, but not by any accession of color. But even those of us who are least observant of skies, know that, irrespective of all supervening colors from the sun, there are white clouds, brown clouds, gray clouds, and black clouds. Are these indeed—what they appear to be—entirely distinct monastic disciplines of cloud: Black Friars, and White Friars, and Friars of Orders Gray? Or is it only their various nearness to us, their denseness, and the failing of the light upon them, that makes some clouds look black[13] and others snowy?

I can only give you qualified and cautious answer. There are, by differences in their own character, Dominican clouds, and there are Franciscan;—there are the Black Hussars of the Bandiera della Morte, and there are the Scots Grays whose horses can run upon the rock. But if you ask me, as I would have you ask me, why argent and why sable, how baptized in white like a bride or a novice, and how hooded with blackness like a Judge of the Vehmgericht Tribunal,—I leave these questions with you, and pass on.

Admitting degrees of darkness, we have next to ask what color, from sunshine can the white cloud receive, and what the black?

You won't expect me to tell you all that, or even the little that is accurately known about that, in a quarter of an hour; yet note these main facts on the matter.

On any pure white, and practically opaque, cloud, or thing like a cloud, as an Alp, or Milan Cathedral, you can have cast by rising or setting sunlight, any tints of amber, orange, or moderately deep rose—you can't have lemon yellows, or any kind of green except in negative hue by opposition; and though by stormlight you may sometimes get the reds cast very deep, beyond a certain limit you cannot go,—the Alps are never vermilion color, nor flamingo color, nor canary color; nor did you ever see a full scarlet cumulus of thundercloud.

On opaque white vapor, then, remember, you can get a glow or a blush of color, never a flame of it.

But when the cloud is transparent as well as pure, and can be filled with light through all the body of it, you then can have by the light reflected[14] from its atoms any force conceivable by human mind of the entire group of the golden and ruby colors, from intensely burnished gold color, through a scarlet for whose brightness there are no words, into any depth and any hue of Tyrian crimson and Byzantine purple. These with full blue breathed between them at the zenith, and green blue nearer the horizon, form the scales and chords of color possible to the morning and evening sky in pure and fine weather; the keynote of the opposition being vermilion against green blue, both of equal tone, and at such a height and acme of brilliancy that you cannot see the line where their edges pass into each other.

No colors that can be fixed in earth can ever represent to you the luster of these cloudy ones. But the actual tints may be shown you in a lower key, and to a certain extent their power and relation to each other.

I have painted the diagram here shown you with colors prepared for me lately by Messrs. Newman, which I find brilliant to the height that pigments can be; and the ready kindness of Mr. Wilson Barrett enables me to show you their effect by a white light as pure as that of the day. The diagram is enlarged from my careful sketch of the sunset of 1st October, 1868, at Abbeville, which was a beautiful example of what, in fine weather about to pass into storm, a sunset could then be, in the districts of Kent and Picardy unaffected by smoke. In reality, the ruby and vermilion clouds were, by myriads, more numerous than I have had time to paint: but the general character of their grouping is well enough expressed. All the illumined clouds are high in the air, and nearly motionless; beneath them, electric storm-cloud rises in a threatening cumulus on the right, and drifts in dark flakes across the horizon, casting from its broken masses radiating shadows on the upper clouds. These shadows are traced, in the first place by making the misty blue of the open sky more transparent, and therefore darker; and secondly, by entirely intercepting the sunbeams on the bars of cloud, which, within the shadowed spaces, show dark on the blue instead of light.

But, mind, all that is done by reflected light—and in that light you never get a *green* ray from the reflecting cloud; there is no such thing in nature as a green lighted cloud relieved from a red sky,—the cloud is always red, and the sky green, and green, observe, by transmitted, not reflected light.

But now note, there is another kind of cloud, pure white, and exquisitely delicate; which acts not by reflecting, nor by refracting, but, as it is now called, *di*ffracting, the sun's rays. The particles of this cloud are said—with what truth I know not[15]—to send the sunbeams round them instead of through them; somehow or other, at any rate, they resolve them into their prismatic elements; and then you have literally a kaleidoscope in the sky, with every color of the prism in absolute purity; but above all in force, now, the ruby red and the *green*,—with purple, and violet-blue, in a virtual equality, more definite than that of the rainbow. The red in the rainbow is mostly brick red, the violet, though beautiful, often lost at the edge; but in the prismatic cloud the violet, the green, and the ruby are all more lovely than in any precious stones, and they are varied as in a bird's breast, changing their places, depths, and extent at every instant.

The main cause of this change being, that the prismatic cloud itself is always in rapid, and generally in fluctuating motion. "A light veil of clouds had drawn itself," says Professor Tyndall, in describing his solitary ascent of Monte Rosa, "between me and the sun, and this was flooded with the most brilliant dyes. Orange, red, green, blue—all the hues produced by diffraction—were exhibited in the utmost splendor.

"Three times during my ascent (the short ascent of the last peak) similar veils drew themselves across the sun, and at each passage the splendid phenomena were renewed. There seemed a tendency to form circular zones of color round the sun; but the clouds were not sufficiently uniform to permit of this, and they were consequently broken into spaces, each steeped with the color due to the condition of the cloud at the place."

Three times, you observe, the veil passed, and three times another came, or the first faded and another formed; and so it is always, as far as I have registered prismatic cloud: and the most beautiful colors I ever saw were on those that flew fastest.

This second diagram is enlarged admirably by Mr. Arthur Severn from my sketch of the sky in the afternoon of the 6th of August, 1880, at Brantwood, two hours before sunset. You are looking west by north, straight towards the sun, and nearly straight towards the wind. From the west the wind blows fiercely towards you out of the blue sky. Under the blue space is a flattened dome of earth-cloud clinging to, and altogether masking the form of, the mountain, known as the Old Man of Coniston.

The top of that dome of cloud is two thousand eight hundred feet above the sea, the mountain two thousand six hundred, the cloud lying two hundred feet deep on it. Behind it, westward and seaward, all's clear; but when the wind out of that blue clearness comes over the ridge of the earth-cloud, at that moment and that line, its own moisture congeals into these white—I believe, *ice*-clouds; threads, and meshes, and tresses, and tapestries, flying, failing, melting, reappearing; spinning and unspinning themselves, coiling and uncoiling, winding and unwinding, faster than eye or thought can follow: and through all their dazzling maze of frosty filaments shines a painted window in palpitation; its pulses of color interwoven in motion, intermittent in fire,—emerald and ruby and pale purple and violet melting into a blue that is not of the sky, but of the sunbeam;—purer than the crystal, softer than the rainbow, and brighter than the snow.

But you must please here observe that while my first diagram did with some adequateness represent to you the color facts there spoken of, the present diagram can only *explain*, not reproduce them. The bright reflected colors of clouds *can* be represented in painting, because they are relieved against darker colors, or, in many cases, *are* dark colors, the vermilion and ruby clouds being often much darker than the green or blue sky beyond them. But in the case of the phenomena now under your attention, the colors are all *brighter than pure white*,—the entire body of the cloud in which they show themselves being white by transmitted light, so that I can only show you what the colors are, and where they are,—but leaving them dark on the white ground. Only artificial, and very high illumination would give the real effect of them,—painting cannot.

Enough, however, is here done to fix in your minds the distinction between those two species of cloud,—one, either stationary,[16] or slow in motion, *reflecting unresolved* light; the other, fast-flying, and *transmitting resolved* light. What difference is there in the nature of the atoms, between those two kinds of clouds? I leave the question with you for to-day, merely hinting to you my suspicion that the prismatic cloud is of finely-comminuted water, or ice,[17] instead of aqueous vapor; but the only clue I have to this idea is in the purity of the rainbow formed in frost mist, lying close to water surfaces. Such mist, however, only becomes prismatic as common rain does, when the sun is behind the spectator, while prismatic clouds are, on the contrary, always between the spectator and the sun.

The main reason, however, why I can tell you nothing yet about these colors of diffraction or interference, is that, whenever I try to find anything firm for you to depend on, I am stopped by the quite frightful inaccuracy of the scientific people's terms, which is the consequence of their always trying to write mixed Latin and English, so losing the grace of the one and the sense of the other. And, in this point of the diffraction of light I am stopped dead by their confusion of idea also, in using the words undulation and vibration as synonyms. "When," says Professor Tyndall, "you are told that the atoms of the sun *vibrate* at different rates, and produce *waves* of different sizes,—your experience of water-waves will enable you to form a tolerably clear notion of what is meant."

'Tolerably clear'!—your toleration must be considerable, then. Do you suppose a water-wave is like a harp-string? Vibration is the movement of a body in a state of tension,—undulation, that of a body absolutely lax. In vibration, not an atom of the body changes its place in relation to another,—in undulation, not an atom of the body remains in the same place with regard to another. In vibration, every particle of the body ignores gravitation, or defies it,—in undulation, every particle of the body is slavishly submitted to it. In undulation, not one wave is like another; in vibration, every pulse is alike. And of undulation itself, there are all manner of visible conditions, which are not true conditions. A flag ripples in the wind, but it does not undulate as the sea does,—for in the sea, the water is taken from the trough to put on to the ridge, but in the flag, though the motion is progressive, the bits of bunting keep their place. You see a field of corn undulating as if it was water,—it is different from the flag, for the ears of corn bow out of their places and return to them,—and yet, it is no more like the undulation of the sea, than the shaking of an aspen leaf in a storm, or the lowering of the lances in a battle.

And the best of the jest is, that after mixing up these two notions in their heads inextricably, the scientific people apply both when neither will fit; and when all undulation known to us presumes weight, and all vibration, impact,—the undulating theory of light is proposed to you concerning a medium which you can neither weigh nor touch!

All *communicable* vibration—of course I mean—and in dead matter: *You* may fall a shivering on your own account, if you like, but you can't get a billiard-ball to fall a shivering on *its* own account.[18]

Yet observe that in thus signalizing the inaccuracy of the terms in which they are taught, I neither accept, nor assail, the conclusions respecting the oscillatory states of light, heat, and sound, which have resulted from the postulate of an elastic, though impalpable and imponderable ether, possessing the elasticity of air. This only I desire you to mark with attention,—that both light and sound are *sensations* of the animal frame, which remain, and must remain, wholly inexplicable, whatever manner of force, pulse, or palpitation may be instrumental in producing them: nor does any such force *become* light or sound, except in its rencontre with an animal. The leaf hears no murmur in the wind to which it wavers on the branches, nor can the clay discern the vibration by which it is thrilled into a ruby. The Eye and the Ear are the creators alike of the ray and the tone;

and the conclusion follows logically from the right conception of their living power,—"He that planted the Ear, shall He not hear? He that formed the Eye, shall not He see?"

For security, therefore, and simplicity of definition of light, you will find no possibility of advancing beyond Plato's "the power that through the eye manifests color," but on that definition, you will find, alike by Plato and all great subsequent thinkers, a *moral* Science of Light founded, far and away more important to you than all the physical laws ever learned by vitreous revelation. Concerning which I will refer you to the sixth lecture which I gave at Oxford in 1872, on the relation of Art to the Science of Light ('The Eagle's Nest'), reading now only the sentence introducing its subject:— "The 'Fiat lux' of creation is therefore, in the deep sense, 'fiat anima,' and is as much, when you understand it, the ordering of Intelligence as the ordering of Vision. It is the appointment of change of what had been else only a mechanical effluence from things unseen to things unseeing,—from Stars, that did not shine, to Earth, that did not perceive,—the change, I say, of that blind vibration into the glory of the Sun and Moon for human eyes: so making possible the communication out of the unfathomable truth of that portion of truth which is good for us, and animating to us, and is set to rule over the day and over the night of our joy and our sorrow."

Returning now to our subject at the point from which I permitted myself, I trust not without your pardon, to diverge; you may incidentally, but carefully, observe, that the effect of such a sky as that represented in the second diagram, so far as it can be abstracted or conveyed by painting at all, implies the total absence of any pervading warmth of tint, such as artists usually call 'tone.' Every tint must be the purest possible, and above all the white. Partly, lest you should think, from my treatment of these two phases of effect, that I am insensible to the quality of tone,—and partly to complete the representation of states of weather undefiled by plague-cloud, yet capable of the most solemn dignity in saddening color, I show you, Diagram 3, the record of an autumn twilight of the year 1845,—sketched while I was changing horses between Verona and Brescia. The distant sky in this drawing is in the glowing calm which is always taken by the great Italian painters for the background of their sacred pictures; a broad field of cloud is advancing upon it overhead, and meeting others enlarging in the distance; these are rain-clouds, which will certainly close over the clear sky, and bring on rain before midnight: but there is no power in them to pollute the sky beyond and above them: they do not darken the air, nor defile it, nor in any way mingle with it; their edges are burnished by the sun like the edges of golden shields, and their advancing march is as deliberate and majestic as the fading of the twilight itself into a darkness full of stars.

These three instances are all I have time to give of the former conditions of serene weather, and of non-electric rain-cloud. But I must yet, to complete the sequence of my subject, show you one example of a good, old-fashioned, healthy, and mighty, storm.

In Diagram 4, Mr. Severn has beautifully enlarged my sketch of a July thundercloud of the year 1858, on the Alps of the Val d'Aosta, seen from Turin, that is to say, some twenty-five or thirty miles distant. You see that no mistake is possible here about what is good weather and what bad, or which is cloud and which is sky; but I show you this sketch especially to give you the scale of heights for such clouds in the atmosphere. These thunder cumuli entirely *hide* the higher Alps. It does not, however, follow that they have buried them, for most of their own aspect of height is owing to the approach of their nearer masses; but at all events, you have cumulus there rising from its base, at about three thousand feet above the plain, to a good ten thousand in the air.

White cirri, in reality parallel, but by perspective radiating, catch the sunshine above, at a height of from fifteen to twenty thousand feet; but the storm on the mountains gathers itself into a full mile's depth of massy cloud, every fold of it involved with thunder, but every form of it, every action, every color, magnificent:—doing its mighty work in its own hour and its own dominion, nor snatching from you for an instant, nor defiling with a stain, the abiding blue of the transcendent sky, or the fretted silver of its passionless clouds.

We so rarely now see cumulus cloud of this grand kind, that I will yet delay you by reading the description of its nearer aspect, in the 'Eagle's Nest.'

"The rain which flooded our fields the Sunday before last, was followed, as you will remember, by bright days, of which Tuesday the 20th (February, 1872) was, in London, notable for the splendor, towards the afternoon, of its white cumulus clouds. There has been so much black east wind lately, and so much fog and artificial gloom, besides, that I find it is actually some two years since I last saw a noble cumulus cloud under full light. I chanced to be standing under the Victoria Tower at Westminster, when the largest mass of them floated past, that day, from the northwest; and I was more impressed than ever yet by the awfulness of the cloud-form, and its unaccountableness, in the present state of our knowledge. The Victoria Tower, seen against it, had no magnitude: it was like looking at Mont Blanc over a lamp-post. The domes of cloud-snow were heaped as definitely: their broken flanks were as gray and firm as rocks, and the whole mountain, of a compass and height in heaven which only became more and more inconceivable as the eye strove to ascend it, was passing behind the tower with a steady march, whose swiftness must in reality have been that of a tempest: yet, along all the ravines of vapor, precipice kept pace with precipice, and not one thrust another.

"What is it that hews them out? Why is the blue sky pure there,—the cloud solid here; and edged like marble: and why does the state of the blue sky pass into the state of cloud, in that calm advance?

"It is true that you can more or less imitate the forms of cloud with explosive vapor or steam; but the steam melts instantly, and the explosive vapor dissipates itself. The cloud, of perfect form, proceeds unchanged. It is not an explosion, but an enduring and advancing presence. The more you think of it, the less explicable it will become to you."

Thus far then of clouds that were once familiar; now at last, entering on my immediate subject, I shall best introduce it to you by reading an entry in my diary which gives progressive description of the most gentle aspect of the modern plague-cloud.

*"Bolton Abbey, 4th July, 1875.*

Half-past eight, morning; the first bright morning for the last fortnight.

At half-past five it was entirely clear, and entirely calm; the moorlands glowing, and the Wharfe glittering in sacred light, and even the thin-stemmed field-flowers quiet as stars, in the peace in which—

'All trees and simples, great and small,That balmy leaf do bear,Than they were painted on a wall,No more do move, nor steir.'

But, an hour ago, the leaves at my window first shook slightly. They are now trembling *continuously*, as those of all the trees, under a gradually rising wind, of which the tremulous action scarcely permits the direction to be defined,—but which falls and returns in fits of varying force, like those which precede a thunderstorm—never wholly ceasing: the direction of its upper current is shown by a few ragged white clouds, moving fast from the north, which rose, at the time of the first leaf-shaking, behind the edge of the moors in the east.

This wind is the plague-wind of the eighth decade of years in the nineteenth century; a period which will assuredly be recognized in future meteorological history as one of phenomena hitherto unrecorded in the courses of nature, and characterized pre-eminently by the almost ceaseless action of this calamitous wind. While I have been writing these sentences, the white clouds above specified have increased to twice the size they had when I began to write; and in about two hours from this time—say by eleven o'clock, if the wind continue,—the whole sky will be dark with them, as it was yesterday, and has been through prolonged periods during the last five years. I first noticed the definite character of this wind, and of the clouds it brings with it, in the year 1871, describing it then in the July number of 'Fors Clavigera'; but little, at that time, apprehending either its universality, or any probability of its annual continuance. I am able now to state positively that its range of power extends from the North of England to Sicily; and that it blows more or less during the whole of the year, except the early autumn. This autumnal abdication is, I hope, beginning: it blew but feebly yesterday, though without intermission, from the north, making every shady place cold, while the sun was burning; its effect on the sky being only to dim the blue of it between masses of ragged cumulus. To-day it has entirely fallen; and there seems hope of bright weather, the first for me since the end of May, when I had two fine days at Aylesbury; the third, May 28th, being black again from morning to evening. There seems to be some reference to the blackness caused by the prevalence of this wind in the old French name of Bise, '*gray* wind'; and, indeed, one of the darkest and bitterest days of it I ever saw was at Vevay in 1872."

The first time I recognized the clouds brought by the plague-wind as distinct in character was in walking back from Oxford, after a hard day's work, to Abingdon, in the early spring of 1871: it would take too long to give you any account this evening of the particulars which drew my attention to them; but during the following months I had too frequent opportunities of verifying my first thoughts of them, and on the first of July in that year wrote the description of them which begins the 'Fors Clavigera' of August, thus:—

"It is the first of July, and I sit down to write by the dismalest light that ever yet I wrote by; namely, the light of this midsummer morning, in mid-England, (Matlock, Derbyshire), in the year 1871.

"For the sky is covered with gray cloud;—not rain-cloud, but a dry black veil, which no ray of sunshine can pierce; partly diffused in mist, feeble mist, enough to make distant objects unintelligible, yet without any substance, or wreathing, or color of its own. And everywhere the leaves of the trees are shaking fitfully, as they do before a thunder-storm; only not violently, but enough to show the passing to and fro of a strange, bitter, blighting wind. Dismal enough, had it been the first morning of its kind that summer had sent. But during all this spring, in London, and at Oxford, through meager March, through changelessly sullen April, through despondent May, and darkened June, morning after morning has come gray-shrouded thus.

"And it is a new thing to me, and a very dreadful one. I am fifty years old, and more; and since I was five, have gleaned the best hours of my life in the sun of spring and summer mornings; and I never saw such as these, till now.

"And the scientific men are busy as ants, examining the sun, and the moon, and the seven stars, and can tell me all about *them*, I believe, by this time; and how they move, and what they are made of.

"And I do not care, for my part, two copper spangles how they move, nor what they are made of. I can't move them any other way than they go, nor make them of anything else, better than they are made. But I would care much and give much, if I could be told where this bitter wind comes from, and what *it* is made of.

"For, perhaps, with forethought, and fine laboratory science, one might make it of something else.

"It looks partly as if it were made of poisonous smoke; very possibly it may be: there are at least two hundred furnace chimneys in a square of two miles on every side of me. But mere smoke would not blow to and fro in that wild way. It looks more to me as if it were made of dead men's souls— such of them as are not gone yet where they have to go, and may be flitting hither and thither, doubting, themselves, of the fittest place for them.

"You know, if there *are* such things as souls, and if ever any of them haunt places where they have been hurt, there must be many about us, just now, displeased enough!"

The last sentence refers of course to the battles of the Franco-German campaign, which was especially horrible to me, in its digging, as the Germans should have known, a moat flooded with waters of death between the two nations for a century to come.

Since that Midsummer day, my attention, however otherwise occupied, has never relaxed in its record of the phenomena characteristic of the plague-wind; and I now define for you, as briefly as possible, the essential signs of it.

1. It is a wind of darkness,—all the former conditions of tormenting winds, whether from the north or east were more or less capable of co-existing with sunlight, and often with steady and bright sunlight; but whenever, and wherever the plague-wind blows, be it but for ten minutes, the sky is darkened instantly.

2. It is a malignant *quality* of wind, unconnected with any one quarter of the compass; it blows indifferently from all, attaching its own bitterness and malice to the worst characters of the proper winds of each quarter. It will blow either with drenching rain, or dry rage, from the south,—with ruinous

blasts from the west,—with bitterest chills from the north,—and with venomous blight from the east.

Its own favorite quarter, however, is the southwest, so that it is distinguished in its malignity equally from the Bise of Provence, which is a north wind always, and from our own old friend, the east.

3. It always blows *tremulously*, making the leaves of the trees shudder as if they were all aspens, but with a peculiar fitfulness which gives them—and I watch them this moment as I write—an expression of anger as well as of fear and distress. You may see the kind of quivering, and hear the ominous whimpering, in the gusts that precede a great thunderstorm; but plague-wind is more panic-struck, and feverish; and its sound is a hiss instead of a wail.

When I was last at Avallon, in South France, I went to see 'Faust' played at the little country theater: it was done with scarcely any means of pictorial effect, except a few old curtains, and a blue light or two. But the night on the Brocken was nevertheless extremely appalling to me,—a strange ghastliness being obtained in some of the witch scenes merely by fine management of gesture and drapery; and in the phantom scenes, by the half-palsied, half-furious, faltering or fluttering past of phantoms stumbling as into graves; as if of not only soulless, but senseless, Dead, moving with the very action, the rage, the decrepitude, and the trembling of the plague-wind.

4. Not only tremulous at every moment, it is also *intermittent* with a rapidity quite unexampled in former weather. There are, indeed, days—and weeks, on which it blows without cessation, and is as inevitable as the Gulf Stream; but also there are days when it is contending with healthy weather, and on such days it will remit for half an hour, and the sun will begin to show itself, and then the wind will come back and cover the whole sky with clouds in ten minutes; and so on, every half-hour, through the whole day; so that it is often impossible to go on with any kind of drawing in color, the light being never for two seconds the same from morning till evening.

5. It degrades, while it intensifies, ordinary storm; but before I read you any description of its efforts in this kind, I must correct an impression which has got abroad through the papers, that I speak as if the plague-wind blew now always, and there were no more any natural weather. On the contrary, the winter of 1878-9 was one of the most healthy and lovely I ever saw ice in;—Coniston lake shone under the calm clear frost in one marble field, as strong as the floor of Milan Cathedral, half a mile across and four miles down; and the first entries in my diary which I read you shall be from the 22d to 26th June, 1876, of perfectly lovely and natural weather.

*"Sunday, 25th June, 1876.*

Yesterday, an entirely glorious sunset, unmatched in beauty since that at Abbeville,—deep scarlet, and purest rose, on purple gray, in bars; and stationary, plumy, sweeping filaments above in upper sky, like '*using up the brush*,' said Joanie; remaining in glory, every moment best, changing from one good into another, (but only in color or light—*form steady*,) for half an hour full, and the clouds afterwards fading into the gray against amber twilight, *stationary in the same form for about two hours*, at least. The darkening rose tint remained till half-past ten, the grand time being at nine.

The day had been fine,—exquisite green light on afternoon hills.

*Monday, 26th June, 1876.*

Yesterday an entirely perfect summer light on the Old Man; Lancaster Bay all clear; Ingleborough and the great Pennine fault as on a map. Divine beauty of western color on thyme and rose,—then twilight of clearest *warm* amber far into night, of *pale* amber all night long; hills dark-clear against it.

And so it continued, only growing more intense in blue and sunlight, all day. After breakfast, I came in from the well under strawberry bed, to say I had never seen anything like it, so pure or intense, in Italy; and so it went glowing on, cloudless, with soft north wind, all day.

*16th July.*

The sunset almost too bright *through the blinds* for me to read Humboldt at tea by,—finally, new moon like a lime-light, reflected on breeze-struck water; traces, across dark calm, of reflected hills."

These extracts are, I hope, enough to guard you against the absurdity of supposing that it all only means that I am myself soured, or doting, in my old age, and always in an ill humor. Depend upon it, when old men are worth anything, they are better humored than young ones; and have learned to see what good there is, and pleasantness, in the world they are likely so soon to have orders to quit.

Now then—take the following sequences of accurate description of thunderstorm, *with* plague-wind.

*"22d June, 1876.*

Thunderstorm; pitch dark, with no *blackness*,—but deep, high, *filthiness* of lurid, yet not sublimely lurid, smoke-cloud; dense manufacturing mist; fearful squalls of shivery wind, making Mr. Severn's sail quiver like a man in a fever fit—all about four, afternoon—but only two or three claps of thunder, and feeble, though near, flashes. I never saw such a dirty, weak, foul storm. It cleared suddenly, after raining all afternoon, at half-past eight to nine, into pure, natural weather,—low rain-clouds on quite clear, green, wet hills.

*Brantwood, 13th August, 1879.*

The most terrific and horrible thunderstorm, this morning, I ever remember. It waked me at six, or a little before—then rolling incessantly, like railway luggage trains, quite ghastly in its mockery of them—the air one loathsome mass of sultry and foul fog, like smoke; scarcely raining at all, but increasing to heavier rollings, with flashes quivering vaguely through all the air, and at last terrific double streams of reddish-violet fire, not forked or zigzag, but rippled rivulets—two at the same instant some twenty to thirty degrees apart, and lasting on the eye at least half a second, with grand artillery-peals following; not rattling crashes, or irregular cracklings, but delivered volleys. It lasted an hour, then passed off, clearing a little, without rain to speak of,—not a glimpse of blue,—and now, half-past seven, seems settling down again into Manchester devil's darkness.

Quarter to eight, morning.—Thunder returned, all the air collapsed into one black fog, the hills invisible, and scarcely visible the opposite shore; heavy rain in short fits, and frequent, though less formidable, flashes, and shorter thunder. While I have written this sentence the cloud has again dissolved itself, like a nasty solution in a bottle, with miraculous and unnatural rapidity, and the hills are in sight again; a double-forked flash—rippled, I mean, like the others—starts into its frightful ladder of light between me and Wetherlam, as I raise my eyes. All black above, a rugged spray cloud on the Eaglet. (The 'Eaglet' is my own name for the bold and elevated crag to the west of the little lake above Coniston mines. It had no name among the country people, and is one of the most conspicuous features of the mountain chain, as seen from Brantwood.)

Half-past eight.—Three times light and three times dark since last I wrote, and the darkness seeming each time as it settles more loathsome, at last stopping my reading in mere blindness. One lurid gleam of white cumulus in upper lead-blue sky, seen for half a minute through the sulphurous chimney-pot vomit of blackguardly cloud beneath, where its rags were thinnest.

*Thursday, 22d Feb. 1883.*

Yesterday a fearfully dark mist all afternoon, with steady, south plague-wind of the bitterest, nastiest, poisonous blight, and fretful flutter. I could scarcely stay in the wood for the horror of it. To-day, really rather bright blue, and bright semi-cumuli, with the frantic Old Man blowing sheaves of lancets and chisels across the lake—not in strength enough, or whirl enough, to raise it in spray, but tracing every squall's outline in black on the silver gray waves, and whistling meanly, and as if on a flute made of a file.

*Sunday, 17th August, 1879.*

Raining in foul drizzle, slow and steady; sky pitch-dark, and I just get a little light by sitting in the bow-window; diabolic clouds over everything: and looking over my kitchen garden yesterday, I found it one miserable mass of weeds gone to seed, the roses in the higher garden putrefied into brown sponges, feeling like dead snails; and the half-ripe strawberries all rotten at the stalks."

6. And now I come to the most important sign of the plague-wind and the plague-cloud: that in bringing on their peculiar darkness, they *blanch* the sun instead of reddening it. And here I must note briefly to you the uselessness of observation by instruments, or machines, instead of eyes. In the first year when I had begun to notice the specialty of the plague-wind, I went of course to the Oxford observatory to consult its registrars. They have their anemometer always on the twirl, and can tell you the force, or at least the pace, of a gale,[19] by day or night. But the anemometer can only record for you how often it has been driven round, not at all whether it went round *steadily*, or went round *trembling*. And on that point depends the entire question whether it is a plague breeze or a healthy one: and what's the use of telling you whether the wind's strong or not, when it can't tell you whether it's a strong medicine, or a strong poison?

But again—you have your *sun*-measure, and can tell exactly at any moment how strong, or how weak, or how wanting, the sun is. But the sun-measurer can't tell you whether the rays are stopped by a dense *shallow* cloud, or a thin *deep* one. In healthy weather, the sun is hidden behind a cloud, as it is behind a tree; and, when the cloud is past, it comes out again, as bright as before. But in plague-wind, the sun is choked out of the whole heaven, all day long, by a cloud which may be a thousand miles square and five miles deep.

And yet observe: that thin, scraggy, filthy, mangy, miserable cloud, for all the depth of it, can't turn the sun red, as a good, business-like fog does with a hundred feet or so of itself. By the plague-wind every breath of air you draw is polluted, half round the world; in a London fog the air itself is pure, though you choose to mix up dirt with it, and choke yourself with your own nastiness.

Now I'm going to show you a diagram of a sunset in entirely pure weather, above London smoke. I saw it and sketched it from my old post of observation—the top garret of my father's house at Herne Hill. There, when the wind is south, we are outside of the smoke and above it; and this diagram, admirably enlarged from my own drawing by my, now in all things best aide-de-camp, Mr. Collingwood, shows you an old-fashioned sunset—the sort of thing Turner and I used to have to look at,—(nobody else ever would) constantly. Every sunset and every dawn, in fine weather, had something of the sort to show us. This is one of the last pure sunsets I ever saw, about the year 1876,—and the point I want you to note in it is, that the air being pure, the smoke on the horizon, though at last it hides the sun, yet hides it through gold and vermilion. Now, don't go away fancying there's any exaggeration in that study. The *prismatic* colors, I told you, were simply impossible to paint; these, which are transmitted colors, can indeed be suggested, but no more. The brightest pigment we have would look dim beside the truth.

I should have liked to have blotted down for you a bit of plague-cloud to put beside this; but Heaven knows, you can see enough of it now-a-days without any trouble of mine; and if you want, in a hurry, to see what the sun looks like through it, you've only to throw a bad half-crown into a basin of soap and water.

Blanched Sun,—blighted grass,—blinded man.—If, in conclusion, you ask me for any conceivable cause or meaning of these things—I can tell you none, according to your modern beliefs; but I can tell you what meaning it would have borne to the men of old time. Remember, for the last twenty years, England, and all foreign nations, either tempting her, or following her, have blasphemed[20] the name of God deliberately and openly; and have done iniquity by proclamation, every man doing as much injustice to his brother as it is in his power to do. Of states in such moral gloom every seer of old predicted the physical gloom, saying, "The light shall be darkened in the heavens thereof, and the stars shall withdraw their shining." All Greek, all Christian, all Jewish prophecy insists on the same truth through a thousand myths; but of all the chief, to former thought, was the fable of the Jewish warrior and prophet, for whom the sun hasted not to go down, with which I leave you to compare at leisure the physical result of your own wars and prophecies, as declared by your own elect journal not fourteen days ago,—that the Empire of England, on which formerly the sun never set, has become one on which he never rises.

What is best to be done, do you ask me? The answer is plain. Whether you can affect the signs of the sky or not, you *can* the signs of the times. Whether you can bring the *sun* back or not, you can assuredly bring back your own cheerfulness, and your own honesty. You may not be able to say to the winds, "Peace; be still," but you can cease from the insolence of your own lips, and the troubling of your own passions.

And all *that* it would be extremely well to do, even though the day *were* coming when the sun should be as darkness, and the moon as blood. But, the paths of rectitude and piety once regained, who shall say that the promise of old time would not be found to hold for us also?—"Bring ye all the tithes into my storehouse, and prove me now herewith, saith the Lord God, if I will not open you the windows of heaven, and pour you out a blessing, that there shall not be room enough to receive it."

# LECTURE II.

*March 11th, 1884.*

It was impossible for me, this spring, to prepare, as I wished to have done, two lectures for the London Institution: but finding its members more interested in the subject chosen than I had anticipated, I enlarged my lecture at its second reading by some explanations and parentheses, partly represented, and partly farther developed, in the following notes; which led me on, however, as I arranged them, into branches of the subject untouched in the former lecture, and it seems to me of no inferior interest.

[1] The vapor over the pool of Anger in the 'Inferno,' the clogging stench which rises from Caina, and the fog of the circle of Anger in the 'Purgatorio' resemble, indeed, the cloud of the Plague-wind very closely,— but are conceived only as supernatural. The reader will no doubt observe, throughout the following lecture, my own habit of speaking of beautiful things as 'natural,' and of ugly ones as 'unnatural.' In the conception of recent philosophy, the world is one Kosmos in which diphtheria is held to be as natural as song, and cholera as digestion. To my own mind, and the more distinctly the more I see, know, and feel, the Earth, as prepared for the abode of man, appears distinctly ruled by agencies of health and disease, of which the first may be aided by his industry, prudence, and piety; while the destroying laws are allowed to prevail against him, in the degree in which he allows himself in idleness, folly, and vice. Had the point been distinctly indicated where the degrees of adversity necessary for his discipline pass into those intended for his punishment, the world would have been put under a manifest theocracy; but the declaration of the principle is at least distinct enough to have convinced all sensitive and earnest persons, from the beginning of speculation in the eyes and mind of Man: and it has been put in my power by one of the singular chances which have always helped me in my work when it was in the right direction, to present to the University of Oxford the most distinct expression of this first principle of mediæval Theology which, so far as I know, exists in fifteenth-century art. It is one of the drawings of the Florentine book which I bought for a thousand pounds, against the British Museum, some ten or twelve years since; being a compendium of classic and mediæval religious symbolism. In the two pages of it, forming one picture, given to Oxford, the delivery of the Law on Sinai is represented on the left hand, (*contrary to the Scriptural narrative,* but in deeper expression of the benediction of the Sacred Law to all nations,) as in the midst of bright and calm light, the figure of the Deity being supported by luminous and level clouds, and

attended by happy angels: while opposite, on the right hand, the worship of the Golden Calf is symbolized by a single decorated pillar, with the calf on its summit, surrounded by the clouds and darkness of a furious storm, issuing from the mouths of fiends;—uprooting the trees, and throwing down the rocks, above the broken tables of the Law, of which the fragments lie in the foreground.

[2] These conditions are mainly in the arrangement of the lower rain-clouds in flakes thin and detached enough to be illuminated by early or late sunbeams: their textures are then more softly blended than those of the upper cirri, and have the qualities of painted, instead of burnished or inflamed, color.

They were thus described in the 4th chapter of the 7th part of 'Modern Painters':—

"Often in our English mornings, the rain-clouds in the dawn form soft level fields, which melt imperceptibly into the blue; or when of less extent, gather into apparent bars, crossing the sheets of broader cloud above; and all these bathed throughout in an unspeakable light of pure rose-color, and purple, and amber, and blue, not shining, but misty-soft, the barred masses, when seen nearer, found to be woven in tresses of cloud, like floss silk, looking as if each knot were a little swathe or sheaf of lighted rain.

"No clouds form such skies, none are so tender, various, inimitable; Turner himself never caught them. Correggio, putting out his whole strength, could have painted them,—no other man."

[3] I did not, in writing this sentence, forget Mr. Gladstone's finely scholastic enthusiasm for Homer; nor Mr. Newton's for Athenian—(I wish it had not been also for Halicarnassian) sculpture. But Byron loved Greece herself—through her death—and *to* his own; while the subsequent refusal of England to give Greece one of our own princes for a king, has always been held by me the most ignoble, cowardly, and lamentable, of all our base commercial *im*policies.

[4] 'Deepening' clouds.—Byron never uses an epithet vainly,—he is the most accurate, and therefore the most powerful, of all modern describers. The deepening of the cloud is essentially necessary to the redness of the orb. Ordinary observers are continually unaware of this fact, and imagine that a red sun can be darker than the sky round it! Thus Mr. Gould, though a professed naturalist, and passing most of his life in the open air, over and over again, in his 'British Birds,' draws the setting sun dark on the sky!

[5] 'Like the blood he predicts.'—The astrological power of the planet Mars was of course ascribed to it in the same connection with its red color. The reader may be interested to see the notice, in 'Modern Painters,' of Turner's

constant use of the same symbol; partly an expression of his own personal feeling, partly, the employment of a symbolic language known to all careful readers of solar and stellar tradition.

"He was very definitely in the habit of indicating the association of any subject with circumstances of death, especially the death of multitudes, by placing it under one of his most deeply *crimsoned* sunset skies.

"The color of blood is thus plainly taken for the leading tone in the storm-clouds above the 'Slave-ship.' It occurs with similar distinctness in the much earlier picture of 'Ulysses and Polypheme,' in that of 'Napoleon at St. Helena,' and, subdued by softer hues, in the 'Old Téméraire.'

"The sky of this Goldau is, in its scarlet and crimson, the deepest in tone of all that I know in Turner's drawings.

"Another feeling, traceable in several of his former works, is an acute sense of the contrast between the careless interests and idle pleasures of daily life, and the state of those whose time for labor, or knowledge, or delight, is passed forever. There is evidence of this feeling in the introduction of the boys at play in the churchyard of Kirkby Lonsdale, and the boy climbing for his kite among the thickets above the little mountain churchyard of Brignal-bank; it is in the same tone of thought that he has placed here the two figures fishing, leaning against these shattered flanks of rock,—the sepulchral stones of the great mountain Field of Death."

[6] 'Thy lore unto calamity.'—It is, I believe, recognized by all who have in any degree become interested in the traditions of Chaldean astrology, that its warnings were distinct,—its promises deceitful. Horace thus warns Leuconoe against reading the Babylonian numbers to learn the time of her death,—he does not imply their promise of previous happiness; and the continually deceptive character of the Delphic oracle itself, tempted always rather to fatal than to fortunate conduct, unless the inquirer were more than wise in his reading. Byron gathers into the bitter question all the sorrow of former superstition, while in the lines italicized, just above, he sums in the briefest and plainest English, all that we yet know, or may wisely think, about the Sun. It is the '*Burning* oracle' (other oracles there are by sound, or feeling, but this by fire) of all that lives; the only means of our accurate knowledge of the things round us, and that affect our lives: it is the *fountain* of all life,—Byron does not say the *origin*;—the origin of life would be the origin of the sun itself; but it is the visible *source* of vital energy, as the spring is of a stream, though the origin is the sea. "And symbol of Him who bestows it."—This the sun has always been, to every one who believes there is a bestower; and a symbol so perfect and beautiful that it may also be thought of as partly an apocalypse.

[7] 'More beautiful in that variety.'—This line, with the one italicized beneath, expresses in Myrrha's mind, the feeling which I said, in the outset, every thoughtful watcher of heaven necessarily had in those old days; whereas now, the variety is for the most part, only in modes of disagreeableness; and the vapor, instead of adding light to the unclouded sky, takes away the aspect and destroys the functions of sky altogether.

[8] 'Steam out of an engine funnel.'—Compare the sixth paragraph of Professor Tyndall's 'Forms of Water,' and the following seventh one, in which the phenomenon of transparent steam becoming opaque is thus explained. "Every bit of steam shrinks, when chilled, to a much more minute particle of water. The liquid particles thus produced form a kind of water dust of exceeding fineness, which floats in the air, and is called a cloud."

But the author does not tell us, in the first place, what is the shape or nature of a 'bit of steam,' nor, in the second place, how the contraction of the individual bits of steam is effected without any diminution of the whole mass of them, but on the contrary, during its steady *expansion*; in the third place he assumes that the particles of water dust are solid, not vesicular, which is not yet ascertained; in the fourth place, he does not tell us how their number and size are related to the quantity of invisible moisture in the air; in the fifth place, he does not tell us how cool invisible moisture differs from hot invisible moisture; and in the sixth, he does not tell us why the cool visible moisture stays while the hot visible moisture melts away. So much for the present state of 'scientific' information, or at least communicativeness, on the first and simplest conditions of the problem before us!

In its wider range that problem embraces the total mystery of volatile power in substance; and of the visible states consequent on sudden—and presumably, therefore, imperfect—vaporization; as the smoke of frankincense, or the sacred fume of modern devotion which now fills the inhabited world, as that of the rose and violet its deserts. What,—it would be useful to know, is the actual bulk of an atom of orange perfume?—what of one of vaporized tobacco, or gunpowder?—and where do *these* artificial vapors fall back in beneficent rain? or through what areas of atmosphere exist, as invisible, though perhaps not innocuous, cloud?

All these questions were put, closely and precisely, four-and-twenty years ago, in the 1st chapter of the 7th part of 'Modern Painters,' paragraphs 4 to 9, of which I can here allow space only for the last, which expresses the final difficulties of the matter better than anything said in this lecture:—

"But farther: these questions of volatility, and visibility, and hue, are all complicated with those of shape. How is a cloud outlined? Granted whatever you choose to ask, concerning its material, or its aspect, its loftiness and luminousness,—how of its limitation? What hews it into a heap, or spins it into a web? Cold is usually shapeless, I suppose, extending over large spaces equally, or with gradual diminution. You cannot have in the open air, angles, and wedges, and coils, and cliffs, of cold. Yet the vapor stops suddenly, sharp and steep as a rock, or thrusts itself across the gates of heaven in likeness of a brazen bar; or braids itself in and out, and across and across, like a tissue of tapestry; or falls into ripples, like sand; or into waving shreds and tongues, as fire. On what anvils and wheels is the vapor pointed, twisted, hammered, whirled, as the potter's clay? By what hands is the incense of the sea built up into domes of marble?"

[9] The opposed conditions of the higher and lower orders of cloud, with the balanced intermediate one, are beautifully seen on mountain summits of rock or earth. On snowy ones they are far more complex: but on rock summits there are three distinct forms of attached cloud in serene weather; the first that of cloud veil laid over them, and *falling* in folds through their ravines, (the obliquely descending clouds of the entering chorus in Aristophanes); secondly, the ascending cloud, which develops itself loosely and independently as it rises, and does not attach itself to the hill-side, while the falling veil cloud clings to it close all the way down;—and lastly the throned cloud, which rests indeed on the mountain summit, with its base, but rises high above into the sky, continually changing its outlines, but holding its seat perhaps all day long.

These three forms of cloud belong exclusively to calm weather; attached drift cloud, (see Note 11) can only be formed in the wind.

[10] 'Glaciers of the Alps,' page 10.—"Let a pound weight be placed upon a cube of granite" (size of supposed cube not mentioned), "the cube is flattened, though in an infinitesimal degree. Let the weight be removed, the cube remains a little flattened. Let us call the cube thus flattened No. 1. Starting with No. 1 as a new mass, let the pound weight be laid upon it. We have a more flattened mass, No. 2.... Apply this to squeezed rocks, to those, for example, which form the base of an obelisk like the Matterhorn,—the conclusion seems inevitable *that the mountain is sinking by its own weight*," etc., etc. Similarly the Nelson statue must be gradually flattening the Nelson column, and in time Cleopatra's needle will be as flat as her pincushion?

[11] 'Glaciers of the Alps,' page 146.—"The sun was near the western horizon, and I remained alone upon the Grat to see his last beams illuminate the mountains, which, with one exception, were without a trace of cloud.

"This exception was the Matterhorn, the appearance of which was extremely instructive. The obelisk appeared to be divided in two halves by a vertical line, drawn from its summit half-way down, to the windward of which we had the bare cliffs of the mountain; and to the left of it a cloud which appeared to cling tenaciously to the rocks.

"In reality, however, there was no clinging; the condensed vapor incessantly got away, but it was ever renewed, and thus a river of cloud had been sent from the mountain over the valley of Aosta. The wind, in fact, blew lightly up the valley of St. Nicholas, charged with moisture, and when the air that held it *rubbed against the cold cone* of the Matterhorn, the vapor was chilled and precipitated in his lee."

It is not explained, why the wind was not chilled by rubbing against any of the neighboring mountains, nor why the cone of the Matterhorn, mostly of rock, should be colder than cones of snow. The phenomenon was first described by De Saussure, who gives the same explanation as Tyndall; and from whom, in the first volume of 'Modern Painters,' I adopted it without sufficient examination. Afterwards I re-examined it, and showed its fallacy, with respect to the cap or helmet cloud, in the fifth volume of 'Modern Painters,' page 124, in the terms given in the subjoined note,[A] but I still retained the explanation of Saussure for the lee-side cloud, engraving in plate 69 the modes of its occurrence on the Aiguille Dru, of which the most ordinary one was afterwards represented by Tyndall in his 'Glaciers of the Alps,' under the title of 'Banner-cloud.' Its less imaginative title, in 'Modern Painters,' of 'Lee-side cloud,' is more comprehensive, for this cloud forms often under the brows of far-terraced precipices, where it has no resemblance to a banner. No true explanation of it has ever yet been given; for the first condition of the problem has hitherto been unobserved,—namely, that such cloud is constant in certain states of weather, under precipitous rocks;—but never developed with distinctness by domes of snow.

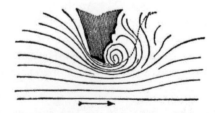

But my former expansion of Saussure's theory is at least closer to the facts than Professor Tyndall's "rubbing against the rocks," and I therefore allow room for it here, with its illustrative wood-cut.

"When a moist wind blows in clear weather over a cold summit, it has not time to get chilled as it approaches the rock, and therefore the air remains clear, and the sky bright on the windward side; but under the lee of the peak, there is partly a back eddy, and partly still air; and in that lull and eddy the wind gets time to be chilled by the rock, and the cloud appears, as a boiling mass of white vapor, rising continually with the return current to the upper edge of the mountain, where it is caught by the straight wind and partly torn, partly melted away in broken fragments.

"In the accompanying figure, the dark mass represents the mountain peak, the arrow the main direction of the wind, the curved lines show the directions of such current and its concentration, and the dotted line encloses the space in which cloud forms densely, floating away beyond and above in irregular tongues and flakes."

[A] "But both Saussure and I ought to have known,—we did know, but did not think of it,—that the covering or cap-cloud forms on hot summits as well as cold ones;—that the red and bare rocks of Mont Pilate, hotter, certainly, after a day's sunshine than the cold storm-wind which sweeps to them from the Alps, nevertheless have been renowned for their helmet of cloud, ever since the Romans watched the cloven summit, gray against the south, from the ramparts of Vindonissa, giving it the name from which the good Catholics of Lucerne have warped out their favorite piece of terrific sacred biography. And both my master and I should also have reflected that if our theory about its formation had been generally true, the helmet cloud ought to form on every cold summit, at the approach of rain, in approximating proportions to the bulk of the glaciers; which is so far from being the case that not only (A) the cap-cloud may often be seen on lower summits of grass or rock, while the higher ones are splendidly clear (which may be accounted for by supposing the wind containing the moisture not to have risen so high); but (B) the cap-cloud always shows a preference for hills of a conical form, such as the Mole or Niesen, which can have very little power in chilling the air, even supposing they were cold themselves; while it will entirely refuse to form huge masses of mountain, which, supposing them of chilly temperament, must have discomforted the atmosphere in their neighborhood for leagues."

[12] See below, on the different uses of the word 'reflection,' note 14, and note that throughout this lecture I use the words 'aqueous molecules,' alike of water liquid or vaporized, not knowing under what conditions or at what temperatures water-dust becomes water-gas; and still less, supposing pure water-gas blue, and pure air blue, what are the changes in either which make them what sailors call "dirty "; but it is one of the worst omissions of the previous lecture, that I have not stated among the characters of the plague-cloud that it is *always* dirty,[A] and *never blue under any conditions,*

neither when deep in the distance, nor when in the electric states which produce sulphurous blues in natural cloud. But see the next note.

[A] In my final collation of the lectures given at Oxford last year on the Art of England, I shall have occasion to take notice of the effect of this character of plague-cloud on our younger painters, who have perhaps never in their lives seen a *clean* sky!

[13] Black clouds.—For the sudden and extreme local blackness of thundercloud, see Turner's drawing of Winchelsea, (England series), and compare Homer, of the Ajaces, in the 4th book of the Iliad,—(I came on the passage in verifying Mr. Hill's quotation from the 5th.)

"ἅμα δὲ νέφος εἴπετο πεζῶν.
Ὡς δ' ὅτ' ἀπὸ σκοπιῆς εἶδεν νέφος αἰπόλος ἀνὴρ
Ἐρχόμενον κατὰ πόντον ὑπὸ Ζεφύροιο ἰωῆς,
Τῷ δέ τ', ἄνευθεν ἔοντι, μελάντερον, ἠΰτε πίσσα
Φαίνετ', ἰὸν κατὰ πόντον, ἄγει δέ τε λαίλαπα πολλήν·
Ῥίγησέν τε ἰδὼν, ὑπό τε σπέος ἤλασε μῆλα·
Τοῖαι ἄμ Αἰάντεσσιν ἀρηϊθόων αἰζηῶν
Δήϊον ἐς πόλεμον πυκιναὶ κίνυντο φάλαγγες
Κυάνεαι,"

I give Chapman's version—noting only that his *breath* of Zephyrus, ought to have been 'cry' or 'roar' of Zephyrus, the blackness of the cloud being as much connected with the wildness of the wind as, in the formerly quoted passage, its brightness with calm of air.

"Behind them hid the groundA cloud of foot, that seemed to smoke. And as a Goatherd spiesOn some hill top, out of the sea a rainy vapor rise,Driven by the breath of Zephyrus, which though far off he rests,Comes on as black as pitch, and brings a tempest in his breastWhereat he, frighted, drives his herds apace into a den;So, darkening earth, with swords and shields, showed these with all their men."

I add here Chapman's version of the other passage, which is extremely beautiful and close to the text, while Pope's is hopelessly erroneous.

"Their ground they still made good,And in their silence and set powers, like fair still clouds they stood,With which Jove crowns the tops of hills in any quiet dayWhen Boreas, and the ruder winds that use to drive awayAir's *dusky vapors*, being *loose*, in many a whistling gale,Are pleasingly bound up and calm, and not a breath exhale."

[14] 'Reflected.'—The reader must be warned in this place of the difference implied by my use of the word 'cast' in page 11, and 'reflected' here: that is

to say, between light or color which an object possesses, whatever the angle it is seen at, and the light which it reverberates at one angle only. The Alps, under the rose[A] of sunset, are exactly of the same color whether you see them from Berne or Schaffhausen. But the gilding to our eyes of a burnished cloud depends, I believe, at least for a measure of its luster, upon the angle at which the rays incident upon it are reflected to the eye, just as much as the glittering of the sea beneath it—or the sparkling of the windows of the houses on the shore.

Previously, at page 10, in calling the molecules of transparent atmospheric 'absolutely' unreflective of light, I mean, in like manner, unreflective from their *surfaces*. Their blue color seen against a dark ground is indeed a kind of reflection, but one of which I do not understand the nature. It is seen most simply in wood smoke, blue against trees, brown against clear light; but in both cases the color is communicated to (or left in) the *transmitted* rays.

So also the green of the sky (p. 13) is said to be given by transmitted light, yellow rays passing through blue air: much yet remains to be known respecting translucent colors of this kind; only let them always be clearly distinguished in our minds from the firmly possessed color of opaque substances, like grass or malachite.

[A] In speaking, at p. 11 of the first lecture, of the limits of depth in the rose-color cast on snow, I ought to have noted the greater strength of the tint possible under the light of the tropics. The following passage, in Mr. Cunningham's 'Natural History of the Strait of Magellan,' is to me of the greatest interest, because of the beautiful effect described as seen on the occasion of his visit to "the small town of Santa Rosa," (near Valparaiso.) "The day, though clear, had not been sunny, so that, although the snowy heights of the Andes had been distinctly visible throughout the greater part of our journey, they had not been illuminated by the rays of the sun. But now, as we turned the corner of a street, the chain of the Cordillera suddenly burst on our gaze in such a blaze of splendor that it almost seemed as if the windows of heaven had been opened for a moment, permitting a flood of *crimson* light to stream forth upon the snow. The sight was so unexpected, and so transcendently magnificent, that a breathless silence fell upon us for a few moments, while even the driver stopped his horses. This deep red glow lasted for three or four minutes, and then rapidly faded into that lovely rosy hue so characteristic of snow at sunset among the Alps."

[15] Diffraction.—Since these passages were written, I have been led, in conversation with a scientific friend, to doubt my statement that the colored portions of the lighted clouds were brighter than the white ones. He was convinced that the resolution of the rays would diminish their

power, and in *thinking* over the matter, I am disposed to agree with him, although my impression at the time has been always that the diffracted colors rose out of the white, as a rainbow does out of the gray. But whatever the facts may be, in this respect the statement in the text of the impossibility of representing diffracted color in painting is equally true. It may be that the resolved hues are darker than the white, as colored panes in a window are darker than the colorless glass, but all are alike in a key which no artifice of painting can approach.

For the rest, the phenomena of diffraction are not yet arranged systematically enough to be usefully discussed; some of them involving the resolution of the light, and others merely its intensification. My attention was first drawn to them near St. Laurent, on the Jura mountains, by the vivid reflection, (so it seemed), of the image of the sun from a particular point of a cloud in the west, after the sun itself was beneath the horizon: but in this image there were no prismatic colors, neither is the constantly seen metamorphosis of pine forests into silver filigree on ridges behind which the sun is rising or setting, accompanied with any prismatic hue; the trees become luminous, but not iridescent: on the other hand, in his great account of his ascent of Mont Blanc with Mr. Huxley, Professor Tyndall thus describes the sun's remarkable behavior on that occasion:—"As we attained the brow which forms the entrance to the Grand Plateau, he *hung his disk upon a spike of rock* to our left, and, surrounded by a glory of interference spectra of the most gorgeous colors, blazed down upon us." ('Glaciers of the Alps,' p. 76.)

Nothing irritates me more, myself, than having the color of my own descriptions of phenomena in anywise attributed by the reader to accidental states either of my mind or body;—but I cannot, for once, forbear at least the innocent question to Professor Tyndall, whether the extreme beauty of these 'interference spectra' may not have been partly owing to the extreme *sobriety* of the observer? no refreshment, it appears, having been attainable the night before at the Grands Mulets, except the beverage diluted with dirty snow, of which I have elsewhere quoted the Professor's pensive report,—"my memory of that tea is not pleasant."

[16] 'Either stationary or slow in motion, reflecting unresolved light.'

The rate of motion is of course not essentially connected with the method of illumination; their connection, in this instance, needs explanation of some points which could not be dealt with in the time of a single lecture.

It is before said, with reserve only, that "a cloud is where it is seen, and is not where it is not seen." But thirty years ago, in 'Modern Painters,' I pointed out (see the paragraph quoted in note 8th), the extreme difficulty of arriving at the cause of cloud outline, or explaining how, if we admitted at any given moment the atmospheric moisture to be generally diffused, it could be chilled by formal *chills* into formal clouds. How, for instance, in the upper cirri, a thousand little chills, alternating with a thousand little warmths, could stand still as a thousand little feathers.

But the first step to any elucidation of the matter is in the firmly fixing in our minds the difference between windless clouds, unaffected by any conceivable local accident, and windy clouds, affected by some change in their circumstances as they move.

In the sunset at Abbeville, represented in my first diagram, the air is absolutely calm at the ground surface, and the motion of its upper currents extremely slow. There is no local reason assignable for the presence of the cirri above, or of the thundercloud below. There is no conceivable cause either in the geology, or the moral character, of the two sides of the town of Abbeville, to explain why there should be decorative fresco on the sky over the southern suburb, and a muttering heap of gloom and danger over the northern. The electric cloud is as calm in motion as the harmless one; it changes its forms, indeed; but imperceptibly; and, so far as can be discerned, only at its own will is exalted, and with its own consent abased.

But in my second diagram are shown forms of vapor sustaining at every instant all kinds of varying local influences; beneath, fastened down by mountain attraction, above, flung afar by distracting winds; here, spread abroad into blanched sheets beneath the sunshine, and presently gathered into strands of coiled cordage in the shade. Their total existence is in metamorphosis, and their every aspect a surprise, or a deceit.

[17] 'Finely comminuted water or *ice*.'

My impression that these clouds were glacial was at once confirmed by a member of my audience, Dr. John Rae, in conversation after the lecture, in which he communicated to me the perfectly definite observations which he has had the kindness to set down with their dates for me, in the following letter:—

"4, ADDISON GARDENS, KENSINGTON, *4th Feb., 1884.*

DEAR SIR,—I have looked up my old journal of thirty years ago, written in pencil because it was impossible to keep ink unfrozen in the snow-hut in which I passed the winter of 1853-4, at Repulse Bay, on the Arctic Circle.[A]

On the 1st of February, 1854, I find the following:—

'A beautiful appearance of some cirrus clouds near the sun, the central part of the cloud being of a fine pink or red, then green, and pink fringe. This continued for about a quarter of an hour. The same was observed on the 27th of the month, but not so bright. Distance of clouds from sun, from 3° to 6°.'

On the 1st February the temperature was 38° below zero, and on the 27th February 26° below.

'On the 23d and 30th (of March) the same splendid appearance of clouds as mentioned in last month's journal was observed. On the first of these days, about 10.30 a.m., it was extremely beautiful. The clouds were about 8° or 10° from the sun, below him and slightly to the eastward,—having a green fringe all round, then pink; the center part at first green, and then pink or red.'

The temperature was 21° below zero, Fahrenheit.

There may have been other colors—blue, perhaps—but I merely noted the most prominent; and what I call green may have been bluish, although I do not mention this last color in my notes.

From the lowness of the temperature at the time, the clouds *must* have been frozen moisture.

The phenomenon is by no means common, even in the Arctic zone.

The second beautiful cloud-picture shown this afternoon brought so visibly to my memory the appearance seen by me as above described, that I could not avoid remarking upon it.

Believe me very truly yours,
JOHN RAE." (M.D., F.R.S.)

Now this letter enables me to leave the elements of your problem for you in very clear terms.

Your sky—altogether—may be composed of one or more of four things:—

Molecules of water in warm weather.
 Molecules of ice in cold weather.
Molecules of water-vapor in warm weather.
Molecules of ice-vapor in cold weather.

But of the size, distances, or modes of attraction between these different kinds of particles, I find no definite information anywhere, except the somewhat vague statement by Sir William Thomson, that "if a drop of water could be magnified so as to be as large as the earth, and have a diameter of eight thousand miles, then a molecule of this water in it would appear *somewhat larger than a shot.*" (What kind of shot?) "*and somewhat smaller than a cricket-ball*"!

And as I finally review the common accounts given of cloud formation, I find it quite hopeless for the general reader to deal with the quantity of points which have to be kept in mind and severally valued, before he can account for any given phenomena. I have myself, in many of the passages of 'Modern Painters' before referred to, conceived of cloud too narrowly as always produced by *cold*, whereas the temperature of a cloud must continually, like that of our visible breath in frosty weather, or of the visible current of steam, or the smoking of a warm lake surface under sudden frost, be above that of the surrounding atmosphere; and yet I never remember entering a cloud without being chilled by it, and the darkness of the plague-wind, unless in electric states of the air, is always accompanied by deadly chill.

Nor, so far as I can read, has any proper account yet been given of the balance, in serene air, of the warm air under the cold, in which the warm air is at once compressed by weight, and expanded by heat, and the cold air is thinned by its elevation, yet contracted by its cold. There is indeed no possibility of embracing the conditions in a single sentence, any more than in a single thought. But the practical balance is effected in calm air, so that its lower strata have no tendency to rise, like the air in a fire balloon, nor its higher strata to fall, unless they congeal into rain or snow.

I believe it will be an extreme benefit to my younger readers if I write for them a little 'Grammar of Ice and Air,' collecting the known facts on all these matters, and I am much minded to put by my ecclesiastical history for a while, in order to relate what is legible of the history of the visible Heaven.

[A] I trust that Dr. Rae will forgive my making the reader better aware of the real value of this communication by allowing him to see also the following passage from the kind private letter by which it was supplemented:—

"Many years in the Hudson's Bay Company's service, I and my men became educated for Arctic work, in which I was five different times employed, in two of which expeditions we lived wholly by our own hunting and fishing for twelve months, once in a stone house (very disagreeable), and another winter in a snow hut (better), *without fire of any kind to warm us.* On the first of these expeditions, 1846-7, my little party, there being no officer but myself, surveyed seven hundred miles of coast of Arctic America by a sledge journey, which Parry, Ross, Bach, and Lyon had failed to accomplish, costing the country about £70,000 or £80,000 at the lowest computation. The total expense of my little party, including my own pay, was under fourteen hundred pounds sterling.

"My Arctic work has been recognized by the award of the founder's gold medal of the Royal Geographical Society (before the completion of the whole of it)."

[18] 'You can't get a billiard ball to fall a shivering on its own account.'—I am under correction in this statement by the Lucasian professor of Cambridge, with respect to the molecules of bodies capable of 'epipolizing' light. "Nothing seems more natural than to suppose that the incident vibrations of the luminiferous ether produce vibratory movements among the ultimate molecules of sensitive substances, and that the molecules in return, *swinging on their own account*, produce vibrations in the luminous ether, and thus cause the sensation of light. The periodic times of these vibrations depend upon the periods in which the molecules are *disposed to swing*." ('On the Changes of Refrangibility of Light,' p. 549.)

It seems to me a pleasant conclusion, this, of recent science, and suggestive of a perfectly regenerate theology. The 'Let there be light' of the former Creation is first expanded into 'Let there be a disposition of the molecules to swing,' and the destinies of mankind, no less than the vitality of the universe, depend thereafter upon this amiable, but perhaps capricious, and at all events not easily influenced or anticipated, disposition!

Is it not also strange that in a treatise entering into so high mathematical analysis as that from which I quote, the false word 'swing,' expressing the action of a body liable to continuous arrest by gravitation, should be employed to signify the oscillation, wholly unaffected by gravity, of substance in which the motion once originated, may cease only with the essence of the body?

It is true that in men of high scientific caliber, such as the writer in this instance, carelessness in expression does not affect the security of their conclusions. But in men of lower rank, mental defects in language indicate fatal flaws in thought. And although the constant habit to which I owe my (often foolishly praised) "command of language"—of never allowing a sentence to pass proof in which I have not considered whether, for the vital word in it, a better could be found in the dictionary, makes me somewhat morbidly intolerant of careless diction, it may be taken for an extremely useful and practical rule, that if a man can think clearly he will write well, and that no good science was ever written in bad English. So that, before you consider whether a scientific author says a true or a false thing, you had better first look if he is able properly to say *any*thing,—and secondly, whether his conceit permits him to say anything properly.

Thus, when Professor Tyndall, endeavoring to write poetically of the sun, tells you that "The Lilies of the field are his workmanship," you may observe, first, that since the sun is not a man, nothing that he does is workmanship; while even the figurative statement that he rejoices *as* a strong man to run his course, is one which Professor Tyndall has no intention whatever of admitting. And you may then observe, in the second place, that, if even in that figurative sense, the lilies of the field are the sun's workmanship, in the same sense the lilies of the hothouse are the stove's workmanship,—and in perfectly logical parallel, you, who are alive here to listen to me, because you have been warmed and fed through the winter, are the workmanship of your own coal-scuttles.

Again, when Mr. Balfour Stewart begins a treatise on the 'Conservation of Energy,' which is to conclude, as we shall see presently, with the prophecy of its total extinction as far as the present world is concerned,—by clothing in a "properly scientific garb," our innocent impression that there is some difference between the blow of a rifle stock and a rifle ball; he prepares for the scientific toilet by telling us in italics that "the something which the rifle ball possesses in contradistinction to the rifle stock is clearly the power of overcoming resistance," since "it can penetrate through oak-wood or through water—or (alas! that it should be so often tried) through the human body; and *this power of penetration*" (italics now mine) "*is the distinguishing characteristic of a substance moving with very great velocity.* Let us define by the term 'Energy,' this power which the rifle ball possesses of overcoming obstacles, or of doing work."

Now, had Mr. Stewart been a better scholar, he would have felt, even if he had not known, that the Greek word 'energy' could only be applied to the living—and of living, with perfect propriety only to the *mental*, action of animals, and that it could no more be applied as a 'scientific garb,' to the flight of a rifle ball, than to the fall of a dead body. And, if he had attained thus much, even of the science of language, it is just possible that the small forte and faculty of thought he himself possesses might have been energized so far as to perceive that the force of all inertly moving bodies, whether rifle stock, rifle ball, or rolling world, is under precisely one and the same relation to their weights and velocities; that the effect of their impact depends—not merely on their pace, but their constitution; and on the relative forms and stability of the substances they encounter, and that there is no more quality of Energy, though much less quality of Art, in the swiftly penetrating shot, or crushing ball, than in the deliberately contemplative and administrative puncture by a gnat's proboscis, or a seamstress' needle.

Mistakes of this kind, beginning with affectations of diction, do not always invalidate general statements or conclusions,—for a bad writer often equivocates out of a blunder as he equivocates into one,—but I have been strict in pointing out the confusions of idea admitted in scientific books between the movement of a swing, that of a sounding violin chord, and that of an agitated liquid, because these confusions have actually enabled Professor Tyndall to keep the scientific world in darkness as to the real nature of glacier motion for the last twenty years; and to induce a resultant quantity of aberration in the scientific mind concerning glacial erosion, of which another twenty years will scarcely undo the damage.

[19] 'Force and pace.'—Among the nearer questions which the careless terminology on which I have dwelt in the above note has left unsettled, I believe the reader will be surprised, as much as I am myself, to find that of the mode of impulse in a common gust of wind! Whence is its strength communicated to it, and how gathered in it? and what is the difference of manner in the impulse between compressible gas and incompressible fluid? For instance: The water at the head of a weir is passing every instant from slower into quicker motion; but (until broken in the air) the fast flowing water is just as dense as the slowly flowing water. But a fan alternately compresses and rarefies the air between it and the cheek, and the violence of a destructive gust in a gale of wind means a momentary increase in velocity and density of which I cannot myself in the least explain,—and find in no book on dynamics explained,—the mechanical causation.

The following letter, from a friend whose observations on natural history for the last seven or eight years have been consistently valuable and instructive to me, will be found, with that subjoined in the note, in various ways interesting; but especially in its notice of the inefficiency of ordinary instrumental registry in such matters:—

"6, MOIRA PLACE, SOUTHAMPTON, *Feb. 8th, 1884.*

DEAR MR. RUSKIN,—Some time since I troubled you with a note or two about sea-birds, etc.... but perhaps I should never have ventured to trouble you again, had not your lecture on the 'Storm Clouds' touched a subject which has deeply interested me for years past. I had, of course, no idea that you had noticed this thing, though I might have known that, living the life you do, you must have done so. As for me, it has been a source of perplexity for years: so much so, that I began to wonder at times whether I was not under some mental delusion about it, until the strange theatrical displays, of the last few months, for which I was more or less prepared, led so many to use their eyes, unmuzzled by brass or glass, for a time. I know you do not bother, or care much to read newspapers, but I have taken the liberty of cutting out and sending a letter of mine, sent on the 1st January to an evening paper,[A] upon this subject, thinking you might like to know that one person, at any rate, has seen that strange, bleared look about the sun, shining so seldom except through a ghastly glare of pale, persistent haze. May it be that the singular coloring of the sunsets marks an end of this long period of plague-cloud, and that in them we have promise of steadier weather? (No: those sunsets were entirely distinct phenomena, and promised, if anything, only evil.—R.)

I was glad to see that in your lecture you gave the dependants upon the instrument-makers a warning. On the 26th I had a heavy sailing-boat lifted and blown, from where she lay hauled up, a distance of four feet, which, as the boat has four hundred-weight of iron upon her keel, gives a wind-gust, or force, not easily measured by instruments.

Believe me, dear Mr. Ruskin,
Yours sincerely,
ROBT. C. LESLIE."

I am especially delighted, in this letter, by my friend's vigorously accurate expression, eyes "unmuzzled by brass or glass." I have had occasion continually, in my art-lectures, to dwell on the great law of human perception and power, that the beauty which is good for us is prepared for the natural focus of the sight, and the sounds which are delightful to us for the natural power of the nerves of the ear; and the art which is admirable in us, is the exercise of our own bodily powers, and not carving by sand-blast, nor oratorizing through a speaking trumpet, nor dancing with spring heels. But more recently, I have become convinced that even in matters of science, although every added mechanical power has its proper use and sphere, yet the things which are vital to our happiness and prosperity can only be known by the rational use and subtle skill of our natural powers. We may trust the instrument with the prophecy of storm, or registry of rainfall; but the conditions of atmospheric change, on which depend the health of animals and fruitfulness of seeds, can only be discerned by the eye and the bodily sense.

Take, for simplest and nearest example, this question of the stress of wind. It is not the actual *power* that is immeasurable, if only it would stand to be measured! Instruments could easily now be invented which would register not only a blast that could lift a sailing boat, but one that would sink a ship of the line. But, lucklessly—the blast won't pose to the instrument! nor can the instrument be adjusted to the blast. In the gale of which my friend speaks in his next letter, 26th January, a gust came down the hill above Coniston village upon two old oaks, which were well rooted in the slate rock, and some fifty or sixty feet high—the one, some twenty yards below the other. The blast tore the highest out of the ground, peeling its roots from the rock as one peels an orange—swept the head of the lower tree away with it in one ruin, and snapped the two leader branches of the upper one over the other's stump, as one would break one's cane over some people's heads, if one got the chance. In wind action of this kind the amount of actual force used is the least part of the business;—it is the suddenness of its concentration, and the lifting and twisting strength, as of a wrestler, which make the blast fatal; none of which elements of storm-power can be recognized by mechanical tests. In my friend's next letter, however, he gives us some evidence of the *consistent* strength of this same gale, and of the electric conditions which attended it:—the prefatory notice of his pet bird I had meant for 'Love's Meinie,' but it will help us through the grimness of our studies here.

*"March 3d, 1884.*

My small blackheaded gull Jack is still flourishing, and the time is coming when I look for that singularly sudden change in the plumage of his head which took place last March. I have asked all my ocean-going friends to note whether these little birds are not the gulls *par excellence* of the sea; and so far all I have heard from them confirms this. It seems almost incredible; but my son, a sailor, who met that hurricane of the 26th of January, writes to me to say that out in the Bay of Biscay on the morning after the gale, 'though it was blowing like blazes, I observed some little gulls of Jacky's species, and they followed us half way across the Bay, seeming to find shelter under the lee of our ship. Some alighted now and then, and rested upon the water as if tired.' When one considers that these birds must have been at sea all that night somewhere, it gives one a great idea of their strength and endurance. My son's ship, though a powerful ocean steamer, was for two whole hours battling head to sea off the Eddystone that night, and for that time the lead gave no increase of soundings, so that she could have made no headway during those two hours; while all the time her yards had the St. Elmo's fire at their ends, looking as though a blue light was burning at each yard-arm, and this was about all they could see.

Yours sincerely,
ROBT. C. LESLIE."

The next letter, from a correspondent with whom I have the most complete sympathy in some expressions of his postscript which are yet, I consider, more for my own private ear than for the public eye, describes one of the more malignant phases of the plague-wind, which I forgot to notice in my lecture.

"BURNHAM, SOMERSET, *February 7th, 1884.*

DEAR SIR,—I read with great interest your first lecture at Oxford on cloud and wind (very indifferently reported in 'The Times'). You have given a name to a wind I've known for years. You call it the plague—I call it the devil-wind: *e. g.*, on April 29th, 1882, morning warmer, then rain storms from east; afternoon, rain squalls; wind, west by south, rough; barometer falling awfully; 4.30 p.m., tremendous wind.—April 30th, all the leaves of the trees, all plants black and dead, as if a fiery blast had swept over them. *All the hedges on windward side black as black tea.*

Another devil-wind came towards the end of last summer. The next day, all the leaves were falling sere and yellow, as if it were late autumn.

I am, dear sir,
Yours faithfully,
A. H. BIRKETT."

I remember both these blights well; they were entirely terrific; but only sudden maxima of the constant morbific power of this wind;—which, if Mr. Birkett saw my *personal* notices of, intercalated among the scientific ones, he would find alluded to in terms quite as vigorously damning as he could desire: and the actual effect of it upon my thoughts and work has been precisely that which would have resulted from the visible phantom of an evil spirit, the absolute opponent of the Queen of the Air,—Typhon against Athena,—in a sense of which I had neither the experience nor the conception when I wrote the illustrations of the myth of Perseus in 'Modern Painters.' Not a word of all those explanations of Homer and Pindar could have been written in weather like that of the last twelve years; and I am most thankful to have got them written, before the shadow came, and I could still see what Homer and Pindar saw. I quote one passage only—Vol. v., p. 141—for the sake of a similitude which reminds me of one more thing I have to say here—and a bit of its note—which I think is a precious little piece, not of word-painting, but of simply told feeling— (*that*, if people knew it, is my real power).

"On the Yorkshire and Derbyshire hills, when the rain-cloud is low and much broken, and the steady west wind fills all space with its strength,[B] the sun-gleams fly like golden vultures; they are flashes rather than shinings; the dark spaces and the dazzling race and skim along the acclivities, and dart and *dip from crag to dell, swallow-like.*"

The dipping of the shadows here described of course is caused only by that of the dingles they cross; but I have not in any of my books yet dwelt enough on the difference of character between the dipping and the mounting winds. Our wildest phase of the west wind here at Coniston is 'swallow-like' with a vengeance, coming down on the lake in swirls which spurn the spray under them as a fiery horse does the dust. On the other hand, the softly ascending winds express themselves in the grace of their cloud motion, as if set to the continuous music of a distant song.[C]

The reader will please note also that whenever, either in 'Modern Painters' or elsewhere, I speak of rate of flight in clouds, I am thinking of it as measured by the horizontal distance overpast in given time, and not as apparent only, owing to the nearness of the spectator. All low clouds appear to move faster than high ones, the pace being supposed equal in both: but when I speak of quick or slow cloud, it is always with respect to a given altitude. In a fine summer morning, a cloud will wait for you among the pines, folded to and fro among their stems, with a branch or two coming out here, and a spire or two there: you walk through it, and look back to it. At another time, on the same spot, the fury of cloud-flood drifts past you like the Rhine at Schaffhausen.

The space even of the doubled lecture does not admit of my entering into any general statement of the action of the plague-cloud in Switzerland and Italy; but I must not omit the following notes of its aspect in the high Alps.

"SALLENCHES, *11th September, 1882.*

This morning, at half-past five, the Mont Blanc summit was clear, and the greater part of the Aiguilles du Plan and Midi clear dark—all, against pure cirri, lighted beneath by sunrise; the sun of course not visible yet from the valley.

By seven o'clock, the plague-clouds had formed in *brown* flakes, down to the base of the Aiguille de Bionassay; entirely covering the snowy ranges; the sun, as it rose to us here, shone only for about ten minutes—gilding in its old glory the range of the Dorons,—before one had time to look from peak to peak of it, the plague-cloud formed from the west, hid Mont Joli, and steadily choked the valley with advancing streaks of dun-colored mist. Now—twenty minutes to nine—there is not *one ray* of sunshine on the whole valley, or on its mountains, from the Forclaz down to Cluse.

These phenomena are only the sequel of a series of still more strange and sad conditions of the air, which have continued among the Savoy Alps for the last eight days, (themselves the sequel of others yet more general, prolonged, and harmful). But the weather was perfectly fine at Dijon, and I doubt not at Chamouni, on the 1st of this month. On the 2d, in the evening, I saw, from the Jura, heavy thunderclouds in the west; on the 3d, the weather broke at Morez, in hot thunder-showers, with intervals of scorching sun; on the 4th, 5th, and 6th there was nearly continuous rain at St. Cergues, the Alps being totally invisible all the time. The sky cleared on the night of the 6th, and on the 7th I saw from the top of the Dole all the western plateaux of Jura quite clearly; but *the entire range of the Alps*, from the Moleson to the Salève, and all beyond,—snow, crag and hill-side,—were wrapped and buried in one unbroken gray-brown winding-sheet, of such cloud *as I had never seen till that day touch an Alpine summit.*

The wind, from the east, (so that it blew *up* over the edge of the Dole cliff, and admitted of perfect shelter on the slope to the west,) was bitter cold, and extremely violent: the sun overhead, bright enough, and remained so during the afternoon; the plague-cloud reaching from the Alps only about as far as the southern shore of the lake of Geneva; but we could not see the Salève; nor even the north shore, farther than to Morges! I reached the Col de la Faucille at sunset, when, for a few minutes, the Mont Blanc and Aiguille Verte showed themselves in dull red light, but were buried again, before the sun was quite down, in the rising deluge of cloud-poison. I saw no farther than the Voirons and Brezon—and scarcely those, during the electric heat of the 9th at Geneva; and last Saturday and Sunday have been mere whirls and drifts of indecisive, but always sullen, storm. This morning I saw the snows clear for the first time, having been, during the whole past week, on steady watch for them.

I have written that the clouds of the 7th were such as I never before saw on the Alps. Often, during the past ten years, I have seen them on my own hills, and in Italy in 1874; but it has always chanced to be fine weather, or common rain and cold, when I have been among the snowy chains; and now from the Dole for the first time I saw the plague-cloud on *them*."

[A] 'THE LOOK OF THE SKY.

'*To the* EDITOR *of the* ST. JAMES'S GAZETTE.

'SIR,—I have been a very constant though not a scientific observer of the sky for a period of forty years; and I confess to a certain feeling of astonishment at the way in which the "recent celestial phenomena" seem to have taken the whole body of scientific observers by surprise. It would even appear that something like these extraordinary sunsets was necessary to call the attention of such observers to what has long been a source of perplexity to a variety of common folk, like sailors, farmers, and fishermen. But to such people the look of the weather, and what comes of that look, is of far more consequence than the exact amount of ozone or the depth or width of a band of the spectrum.

'Now, to all such observers, including myself, it has been plain that of late neither the look of the sky nor the character of the weather has been, as we should say, what it used to be; and those whose eyes were strong enough to look now and then toward the sun have noticed a very marked increase of what some would call a watery look about him, which might perhaps be better expressed as a white sheen or glare, at times developing into solar halo or mock suns, as noted in your paper of the 2d of October last year. A fisherman would describe it as "white and davery-like." So far as my observation goes, this appearance was only absent here for a limited period during the present summer, when we had a week or two of nearly normal weather; the summer before it was seldom absent.

'Again, those whose business or pleasure has depended on the use of wind-power have all remarked the strange persistence of hard westerly and easterly winds, the westerly ones at times partaking of an almost trade-wind-like force and character. The summer of 1882 was especially remarkable for these winds, while each stormy November has been followed by a period about mid-winter of mild calm weather with dense fog. During these strong winds in summer and early autumn the weather would remain bright and sunny, and to a landsman would be not remarkable in any way, while the barometer has been little affected by them; but it has been often observed by those employed on the water that when it ceased blowing half a gale the sky at once became overcast, with damp weather or rain. This may all seem common enough to most people; but to those accustomed to gauge the wind by the number of reefs wanted in a mainsail or foresail it was not so; and the number of consecutive days when two or more reefs have been kept tied down during the last few summers has been remarkable—alternating at times with equally persistent spells of calm and fog such as we are now passing through. Again, we have had an unusually early appearance of ice in the Atlantic, and most abnormal weather over Central Europe; while in a letter I have just received from an old hand on board a large Australian clipper, he speaks of heavy gales and big seas off that coast in almost the height of their summer.

'Now, upon all this, in our season of long twilights, we have bursting upon us some clear weather; with a display of cloud-forms or vapor at such an elevation that, looking at them one day through an opening in the nearer clouds, they seemed so distant as to resemble nothing but the delicate grain of ivory upon a billiard-ball. And yet with the fact that two-thirds of this earth is covered with water, and bearing in mind the effect which a very small increase of sun-power would have in producing cloud and lifting it above its normal level for a time, we are asked to believe that this sheen is all dust of some kind or other, in order to explain what are now known as the "recent sunsets": though I venture to think that we shall see more of them yet when the sun comes our way again.

'At first sight, increased sun-power would seem to mean more sunshine; but a little reflection would show us that this would not be for long, while any considerable addition to the sun's power would be followed by such a vast increase of vapor that we should only see him, in our latitudes, at very short intervals. I am aware that all this is most unscientific; but I have read column after column of explanation written by those who are supposed to know all about such things, and find myself not a jot the wiser for it. Do you know anybody who is?—I am, Sir, your obedient servant,

'AN UNSCIENTIFIC OBSERVER. (R. LESLIE.)
*January 1.*'

[B] "I have been often at great heights on the Alps in rough weather, and have seen strong gusts of storm in the plains of the south. But, to get full expression of the very heart and meaning of wind, there is no place like a Yorkshire moor. I think Scottish breezes are thinner, very bleak and piercing, but not substantial. If you lean on them they will let you fall, but one may rest against a Yorkshire breeze as one would on a quickset hedge. I shall not soon forget,—having had the good fortune to meet a vigorous one on an April morning, between Hawes and Settle, just on the flat under Wharnside,—the vague sense of wonder *with which I watched Ingleborough stand without rocking.*"

[C] Compare Wordsworth's

"Oh beauteous birds, methinks ye measureYour movements to some heavenly tune."

And again—

"While the mists,Flying and rainy vapors, call out shapes,And phantoms from the crags and solid earth,As fast as a musician scatters soundsOut of an instrument."

And again—

"The Knight had ridden down from Wensley moor,With the slow motion of a summer cloud."

[20] 'Blasphemy.'—If the reader can refer to my papers on Fiction in the 'Nineteenth Century,' he will find this word carefully defined in its Scriptural, and evermore necessary, meaning,—'Harmful speaking'—not against God only, but against man, and against all the good works and

purposes of Nature. The word is accurately opposed to 'Euphemy,' the right or well-speaking of God and His world; and the two modes of speech are those which going out of the mouth sanctify or defile the man.

Going out of the mouth, that is to say, deliberately and of purpose. A French postilion's 'Sacr-r-ré'—loud, with the low 'Nom de Dieu' following between his teeth, is not blasphemy, unless against his horse;—but Mr. Thackeray's close of his Waterloo chapter in 'Vanity Fair,' "And all the night long Amelia was praying for George, who was lying on his face dead with a bullet through his heart," is blasphemy of the most fatal and subtle kind.

And the universal instinct of blasphemy in the modern vulgar scientific mind is above all manifested in its love of what is ugly, and natural inthrallment by the abominable;—so that it is ten to one if, in the description of a new bird, you learn much more of it than the enumerated species of vermin that stick to its feathers; and in the natural history museum of Oxford, humanity has been hitherto taught, not by portraits of great men, but by the skulls of cretins.

But the *deliberate* blasphemy of science, the assertion of its own virtue and dignity against the always implied, and often asserted, vileness of all men and—Gods,—heretofore, is the most wonderful phenomenon, so far as I can read or perceive, that hitherto has arisen in the always marvelous course of the world's mental history.

Take, for brief general type, the following 92d paragraph of the 'Forms of Water':—

"But while we thus acknowledge our limits, there is also reason for wonder at the extent to which Science has mastered the system of nature. From age to age and from generation to generation, fact has been added to fact and law to law, the true method and order of the Universe being thereby more and more revealed. In doing this, Science has encountered and overthrown various forms of superstition and deceit, of credulity and imposture. But the world continually produces weak persons and wicked persons, and as long as they continue to exist side by side, as they do in this our day, very debasing beliefs will also continue to infest the world."

The debasing beliefs meant being simply those of Homer, David, and St. John[A]—as against a modern French gamin's. And what the results of the intended education of English gamins of every degree in that new higher theology will be, England is I suppose by this time beginning to discern.

In the last 'Fors'[B] which I have written, on education of a safer kind, still possible, one practical point is insisted on chiefly,—that learning by heart, and repetition with perfect accent and cultivated voice, should be made quite principal branches of school discipline up to the time of going to the university.

And of writings to be learned by heart, among other passages of indisputable philosophy and perfect poetry, I include certain chapters of the—now for the most part forgotten—wisdom of Solomon; and of these, there is one selected portion which I should recommend not only school-boys and girls, but persons of every age, if they don't know it, to learn forthwith, as the shortest summary of Solomon's wisdom;—namely, the seventeenth chapter of Proverbs, which being only twenty-eight verses long, may be fastened in the dullest memory at the rate of a verse a day in the shortest month of the year. Out of the twenty-eight verses, I will read you seven, for example of their tenor,—the last of the seven I will with your good leave dwell somewhat upon. You have heard the verses often before, but probably without remembering that they are all in this concentrated chapter.

1.  Verse 1.—Better is a dry morsel, and quietness therewith, than a house full of good eating, with strife.

(Remember, in reading this verse, that though England has chosen the strife, and set every man's hand against his neighbor, her house is not yet so full of good eating as she expected, even though she gets half of her victuals from America.)

2.  Verse 3.—The fining pot is for silver, the furnace for gold, but the Lord tries the heart.

(Notice the increasing strength of trial for the more precious thing: only the melting-pot for the silver—the fierce furnace for the gold—but the Fire of the Lord for the heart.)

3.  Verse 4.—A wicked doer giveth heed to false lips.

(That means, for *you*, that, intending to live by usury and swindling, you read Mr. Adam Smith and Mr. Stuart Mill, and other such political economists.)

4.  Verse 5.—Whoso mocketh the poor, reproacheth his Maker.

(Mocketh,—by saying that his poverty is his fault, no less than his misfortune,—England's favorite theory now-a-days.)

5.  Verse 12.—Let a bear robbed of her whelps meet a man, rather than a fool in his folly.

(Carlyle is often now accused of false scorn in his calling the passengers over London Bridge, "mostly fools,"—on the ground that men are only to be justly held foolish if their intellect is under, as only wise when it is above, the average. But the reader will please observe that the essential function of modern education is to develop what capacity of mistake a man has. Leave him at his forge and plow,—and those tutors teach him his true value, indulge him in no error, and provoke him to no vice. But take him up to London,—give him her papers to read, and her talk to hear,—and it is fifty to one you send him presently on a fool's errand over London Bridge.)

6.     Now listen, for this verse is the question you have mainly to ask yourselves about your beautiful all-over-England system of competitive examination:—

Verse 16. Wherefore is there a price in the hand of a fool to get wisdom, seeing he hath no heart to it?

(You know perfectly well it isn't the wisdom you want, but the "station in life,"—and the money!)

7.     Lastly, Verse 7.—Wisdom is before him that hath understanding, but the eyes of a fool are in the ends of the earth.

"And in the beginnings of it"! Solomon would have written, had he lived in our day; but we will be content with the ends at present. No scientific people, as I told you at first, have taken any notice of the more or less temporary phenomena of which I have to-night given you register. But, from the constant arrangements of the universe, the same respecting which the thinkers of former time came to the conclusion that they were essentially good, and to end in good, the modern speculator arrives at the quite opposite and extremely uncomfortable conclusion that they are essentially evil, and to end—in nothing.

And I have here a volume,[C] before quoted, by a very foolish and very lugubrious author, who in his concluding chapter gives us,—founded, you will observe, on a series of 'ifs,'—the latest scientific views concerning the order of creation. "We have spoken already about a medium pervading space"—this is the Scientific God, you observe, differing from the unscientific one, in that the purest in heart cannot see—nor the softest in heart feel—this spacious Deity—a *Medium*, pervading space—"the office of which" (italics all mine) "appears to be to *degrade* and ultimately *extinguish*, all differential motion. It has been well pointed out by Thomson, that, looked at *in this light*, the universe is a system that had a beginning and must have an end, for a process of degradation cannot be eternal. If we could view the Universe as a candle not lit, then it is perhaps conceivable to regard it as having been always in existence; but if we regard it rather as a candle that has been lit, we become absolutely certain that it cannot have been burning from eternity, and that a time will come when it will cease to burn. We are led to look to a beginning in which the particles of matter were in a diffuse chaotic state, but endowed with the power of gravitation; and we are led to look to an end in which the whole Universe will be one equally heated inert mass, *and from which everything like life, or motion, or beauty, will have utterly gone away*."

Do you wish me to congratulate you on this extremely cheerful result of telescopic and microscopic observation, and so at once close my lecture? or may I venture yet to trespass on your time by stating to you any of the more comfortable views held by persons who did not regard the universe in what my author humorously calls "this *light*"?

In the peculiarly characteristic notice with which the 'Daily News' honored my last week's lecture, that courteous journal charged me, in the metaphorical term now classical on Exchange, with "hedging," to conceal my own opinions. The charge was not prudently chosen, since, of all men now obtaining any portion of popular regard, I am pretty well known to be precisely the one who cares least either for hedge or ditch, when he chooses to go across country. It is certainly true that I have not the least mind to pin my heart on my sleeve, for the daily daw, or nightly owl, to peck at; but the essential reason for my not telling you my own opinions on this matter is—that I do not consider them of material consequence to you.

It *might* possibly be of some advantage for you to know what—were he now living, Orpheus would have thought, or Æschylus, or a Daniel come to judgment, or John the Baptist, or John the Son of Thunder; but what either you, or I, or any other Jack or Tom of us all, think,—even if we knew what to think,—is of extremely small moment either to the Gods, the clouds, or ourselves.

Of myself, however, if you care to hear it, I will tell you thus much: that had the weather when I was young been such as it is now, no book such as 'Modern Painters' ever would or *could* have been written; for every argument, and every sentiment in that book, was founded on the personal experience of the beauty and blessing of nature, all spring and summer long; and on the then demonstrable fact that over a great portion of the world's surface the air and the earth were fitted to the education of the spirit of man as closely as a school-boy's primer is to his labor, and as gloriously as a lover's mistress is to his eyes.

That harmony is now broken, and broken the world round: fragments, indeed, of what existed still exist, and hours of what is past still return; but month by month the darkness gains upon the day, and the ashes of the Antipodes glare through the night.[D]

What consolation, or what courage, through plague, danger, or darkness, you can find in the conviction that you are nothing more than brute beasts driven by brute forces, your other tutors can tell you—not I: but *this* I can tell you—and with the authority of all the masters of thought since time was time,—that, while by no manner of vivisection you can learn what a *Beast* is, by only looking into your own hearts you may know what a *Man* is,—and know that his only true happiness is to live in Hope of something to be won by him, in Reverence of something to be worshiped by him, and in Love of something to be cherished by him, and cherished—forever.

Having these instincts, his only rational conclusion is that the objects which can fulfill them may be by his effort gained, and by his faith discerned; and his only earthly wisdom is to accept the united testimony of the men who have sought these things in the way they were commanded. Of whom no single one has ever said that his obedience or his faith had been vain, or found himself cast out from the choir of the living souls, whether here, or departed, for whom the song was written:—

God be merciful unto us, and bless us, and cause His face to shine upon us;That Thy way may be known upon earth, Thy saving health among all nations.

Oh let the nations rejoice and sing for joy, for Thou shalt judge the people righteously and govern the nations upon earth.*Then* shall the earth yield her increase, and God, even our own God, shall bless us.God shall bless us, and all the ends of the earth shall fear Him.

[A] With all who died in Faith, not having received the Promises, nor— according to your modern teachers—ever to receive.

[B] Hence to the end the text is that read in termination of the lecture on its second delivery, only with an added word or two of comment on Proverbs xvii.

[C] 'The Conservation of Energy.' King and Co., 1873.

[D] Written under the impression that the lurid and prolonged sunsets of last autumn had been proved to be connected with the flight of volcanic ashes. This has been since, I hear, disproved again. Whatever their cause, those sunsets were, in the sense in which I myself use the word, altogether 'unnatural' and terrific: but they have no connection with the far more fearful, because protracted and increasing, power of the Plague-wind. The letter from White's 'History of Selborne,' quoted by the Rev. W. R. Andrews in his letter to the 'Times,' (dated January 8th) seems to describe aspects of the sky like these of 1883, just a hundred years before, in 1783: and also some of the circumstances noted, especially the variation of the wind to all quarters without alteration in the air, correspond with the character of the plague-wind; but the fog of 1783 made the sun dark, with iron-colored rays—not pale, with blanching rays. I subjoin Mr. Andrews' letter, extremely valuable in its collation of the records of simultaneous volcanic phenomena; praying the reader also to observe the instantaneous acknowledgment, by the true 'Naturalist,' of horror in the violation of beneficent natural law.

"THE RECENT SUNSETS AND VOLCANIC ERUPTIONS."

"SIR,—It may, perhaps, be interesting at the present time, when so much attention has been given to the late brilliant sunsets and sunrises, to be reminded that almost identically the same appearances were observed just a hundred years ago.

Gilbert White writes in the year 1783, in his 109th letter, published in his 'Natural History of Selborne':—

'The summer of the year 1783 was an amazing and portentous one, and full of horrible phenomena; for besides the alarming meteors and tremendous thunderstorms that affrighted and distressed the different counties of this kingdom, the peculiar haze or smoky fog that prevailed for many weeks in this island and in every part of Europe, and even beyond its limits, was a most extraordinary appearance, unlike anything known within the memory of man. By my journal I find that I had noticed this strange occurrence from June 23d to July 20th inclusive, during which period the wind varied to every quarter without making any alteration in the air. The sun at noon looked as black as a clouded moon, and shed a ferruginous light on the ground and floors of rooms, but was particularly lurid and blood-colored at rising and setting. The country people began to look with a superstitious awe at the red lowering aspect of the sun; and, indeed, there was reason for the most enlightened person to be apprehensive, for all the while Calabria and part of the Isle of Sicily were torn and convulsed with earthquakes, and about that juncture a volcano sprang out of the sea on the coast of Norway.'

Other writers also mention volcanic disturbances in this same year, 1783. We are told by Lyell and Geikie, that there were great volcanic eruptions in and near Iceland. A submarine volcano burst forth in the sea, thirty miles southwest of Iceland, which ejected so much pumice that the ocean was covered with this substance, to the distance of 150 miles, and ships were considerably impeded in their course; and a new island was formed, from which fire and smoke and pumice were emitted.

Besides this submarine eruption, the volcano Skaptar-Jökull, on the mainland, on June 11th, 1783, threw out a torrent of lava, so immense as to surpass in magnitude the bulk of Mont Blanc, and ejected so vast an amount of fine dust, that the atmosphere over Iceland continued loaded with it for months afterwards. It fell in such quantities over parts of Caithness—a distance of 600 miles—as to destroy the crops, and that year is still spoken of by the inhabitants as the year of 'the ashie.'

These particulars are gathered from the text-books of Lyell and Geikie.

I am not aware whether the coincidence in time of the Icelandic eruptions, and of the peculiar appearance of the sun, described by Gilbert White, has yet been noticed; but this coincidence may very well be taken as some little evidence towards explaining the connection between the recent beautiful sunsets and the tremendous volcanic explosion of the Isle of Krakatoa in August last.

W. R. ANDREWS, F. G. S.
Teffont Ewyas Rectory, Salisbury, January 8th."

Milton Keynes UK
Ingram Content Group UK Ltd.
UKHW030749221024
449869UK00004B/253